Proceeding of...

Lean Software & Systems Conference 2011

Edited by Eric Willeke

BLUE
HOLE
PRESS

Sequim, Washington

Blue Hole Press
72 Buckhorn Road
Sequim, WA 98382

www.blueholepress.com

Proceeding of Lean Software and Systems Conference 2011

Library of Congress Cataloging-in-Publication Data applied for. Available at www.loc.gov

ISBN: 978-0-9845214-9-4

Cover design by Christopher Uryga of Aedis Creative.

Content editing by Tonya Murphy.

The Lean Software and Systems Consortium
appreciates these organizations for their contributions
making LSSC11 and these proceedings possible.

Dear Lean Enthusiast,

Your participation in the Lean Software and Systems Consortium is a direct investment in the thought leadership that drives Lean practices forward. The annual conference is the premiere opportunity for each of us to learn, explore, and share our continually improving understanding of the concepts that prove to be a new, better way of producing high-quality software.

Throughout the past few years, this community and its leadership has worked continually to increase public recognition of the next generation of methods, processes, and organization for software and systems engineering development. The collective knowledge we bring to our conversations is what leads us to the next level of understanding, allowing us to guide our organizations to success.

Unfortunately, the immense value of these conversations cannot easily live beyond the few short days of the conference. Thus, Rally Software is especially happy to sponsor this collection of the authors' thoughts and perspectives, the body of evidence and experience that demonstrates both the successes and failures using our newly understood techniques. This willingness to accept, embrace, and learn from failure is one of the forces that drives Lean and kanban forward!

We at Rally look forward to the developments that will come from this year's conference. The future of Agile and Lean depends on you and your peers to pave the way and lead us all to the next phase. Thank you for joining us!

Ryan Martens

CTO & Founder - Rally Software

Table of Contents

Leaning Towards a Software Factory
  by Jeff Anderson, Alexis Hui, and Anthony Chan..1

Using Kanban to Achieve Rapid Maturity in Configuration Management
  by Paul Anderson and Dennis Stevens..13

From Scrum to Flow at Xbox IT by Phllip Cave..23

Software Development with Human Values, Powered by Kanban
  by Carlos Churba and Ricardo Colusso..31

Outside-In Risk Management by Julian Everett.. 37

Leaner Programmer Anarchy by Fred George and Antonio Torreno...........................49

Using Class of Service to Manage Risk in Innovative New Product Development
  by Siddharta Govindaraj and Sreekanth Tadipatri......................................57

Organic, not Chaotic: How to Grow your Architecture by Liz Keogh........................ 65

Nothing to Hide, Nowhere to Run by Jason Little... 75

Value Innovation for Accelerated Competitive Advantage and Organizational
  Maturity by Masa Kevin Maeda...87

Managing and Visualizing Non-linear Workflows Using a Kanban Matrix
  by Gerard Meszaros..99

Gemba Walks and Visual Management by Inbar Oren... 111

Kanban in a CMMI ML3 Environment by Andrea Pinto and Felipe Furtado.................. 117

Boyd's OODA Loop: Not What You Think by Chet Richards..................................... 127

Kanban System Archtypes by Karl Scotland...137

Lean Software Development Comes of Age by Alan Shalloway............................143

A Large Kanban Implementation by Jasper Sonnevelt...151

Leading Your Business Customer: A Case Study of A3 Thinking and why it Works
  by Dean C. Stevens...157

Lean Systems Engineering within System Design Activities
  by Richard Turner and Jon Wade...169

Using Flow Approaches to Effectively Manage Agile Testing by Yuval Yeret..................177

Innovation as a Science by Greg Yezersky...185

Leaning Towards a Software Factory

by

Jeff Anderson, jeffanderson@deloitte.ca

Alexis Hui, alhui@deloitte.ca

Anthony Chan, anthchan@deloitte.ca

ABSTRACT

This paper will describe Deloitte's experience in assisting its clients in conceptualizing, designing, and executing the vision of running IT application delivery based on the metaphor of a software factory. The presentation will describe the journey that we took with our clients to create a delivery model based on Lean principles and practices. This delivery model included process, organization, tools, and financial components. The journey starts at the vision articulation stage, through the factory design, and into referencing and adoption. Topics covered include usage of value stream, enterprise Kanban, organizational design, change management, a flow-based work package framework, and the creation of a financial and process framework based on distinct work types.

THE NEED FOR BETTER DELIVERY OUTCOMES

Clearly Not Having the Desired Outcomes

The Ontario Public Service (OPS), like most government organizations, is broken up into explicit departments, each with a defined scope of responsibility. At one point in time, each ministry within the OPS had a dedicated IT organization that would service its development and operational needs. The OPS underwent a wave of consolidation, grouping various IT organizations into "clusters". Each cluster would service a group of similar but still unique ministries. One such example of a cluster is the "The Children, Youth and Social Services Cluster", responsible for servicing the Ministry of Children and Youth Services as well as the Ministry of Social Services.

The intent of this consolidation was to get control of soaring IT costs and gain efficiency through rationalization. It was also expected that this rationalization would lead to quicker delivery turnaround time. While exact data is scarce, there certainly is a consensus among many within the OPS that this consolidation did not produce the desired outcomes of lower cost and more efficient delivery. There's also a perception of substantial decline in overall service responsiveness.

Increasingly these IT clusters have had an interest in looking at new models and new approaches that would support better rationalization while not sacrificing delivery cycle time. In some instances, various clusters have turned towards lean thinking as a source of inspiration to enable change.

Grassroots Approach to Change within the Public Sector?

The old approach to rationalization within the OPS was to legislate and enforce it. As an example infrastructure, including support, was rationalized into one agency; all clusters had to use this agency for infrastructure related reasons. All ministries were also mandated to use the IT cluster assigned to them for application delivery, software, and other IT services. This mandated approach to service usage had adverse impacts on responsiveness and performance.

The new approach to rationalization leverages a more grassroots model. Different clusters are now volunteering to become centers of excellence (COE) for specific services. Examples include a Case Management COE, a Java COE, and a .Net COE. Usage of these COEs by various ministries would not be mandatory, but by choice, and based on the desire for improved outcomes. We have worked with multiple clusters building these COEs to update their delivery models based on a "delivery factory" metaphor.

GETTING THE VISION RIGHT FOR LARGE-SCALE CHANGE

Engaging Leadership

We have worked with three separate clusters starting the redefinition of their delivery organization based on a delivery factory metaphor. In most of these situations the first big challenge came from the factory metaphor itself. In many of our clients' minds a factory model implied a more commoditized approach to delivery, more specialization, more standardized processes, rationalized toolsets, more top-down control, and more overall bureaucracy. We did not feel that we were in the position to encourage our clients to abandon this metaphor outright. Instead, we elected to look at the valuable aspects of the factory metaphor as it applied to software product delivery and towards a common understanding of these activities. When meeting with executives to define this common understanding we were faced with another challenge, a common perception which could be best described as "my upstream consumer is unable to prioritize anything, my downstream supplier provides a horrible service, and I am about as efficient as could possibly be." Needless to say, our team had its work cut out if we were to change leadership perception of the change required to improve.

Engaging Everyone Else

On one of our engagements, articulation of a common understanding was assisted by us being allowed to facilitate three weeks' worth of value stream mapping sessions. We invited approximately 50 to 60 staff members to attend 18 separate sessions.

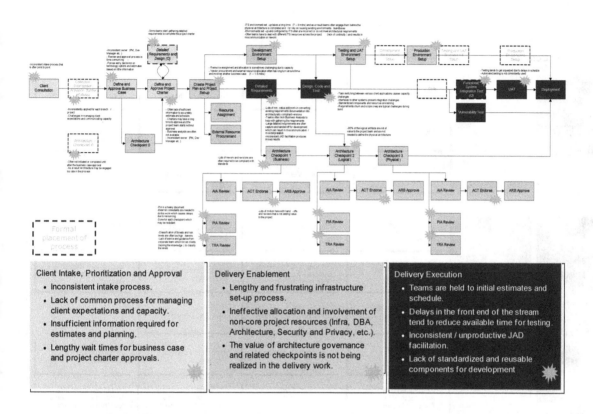

Client Intake, Prioritization and Approval	Delivery Enablement	Delivery Execution
• Inconsistent intake process. • Lack of common process for managing client expectations and capacity. • Insufficient information required for estimates and planning. • Lengthy wait times for business case and project charter approvals.	• Lengthy and frustrating infrastructure set-up process. • Ineffective allocation and involvement of non-core project resources (Infra, DBA, Architecture, Security and Privacy, etc.). • The value of architecture governance and related checkpoints is not being realized in the delivery work.	• Teams are held to initial estimates and schedule. • Delays in the front end of the stream tend to reduce available time for testing. • Inconsistent / unproductive JAD facilitation. • Lack of standardized and reusable components for development

The sessions were incredibly informative, revealing obvious problems such as a cumbersome architecture gating process, as well as reviewing issues that the senior manager was completely unaware of. In one case, a developer had lost the ability to debug on a specific environment due to the loss of access to a debugging tool, with no resolution in sight for over six months. A leadership value stream mapping session was then conducted exclusively for the executives and results were compared. Most of the leadership group was astounded by the bottlenecks, impediments, and other issues being experienced by ground-level staff. This helped establish a common understanding of the challenges and gaps facing the organization. It also allowed us to work with leadership to frame the delivery capabilities needed to help transition the organization into a delivery factory, one based on lean principles such as employee empowerment, collaboration, limiting work in progress, and test driven approaches.

Components — **Capabilities**

	Components	Capabilities			
Solutions Storefront	Customer Engagement	Client Engagement and Interaction Model	Joint Client and Cluster Strategic Planning	Client Forecasting and Demand Analysis	Solution Catalogue Marketing
	Portfolio Management	Portfolio – Solution Triage Process	Client Prioritization and Requirements Breakdown Process	Cluster Supply Analysis and Forecasting	Portfolio and Product Roadmaps and Dashboards
	Solutions Catalogue Offering	Solutions Catalogue and Reference Architectures	Assessment of New / Existing Vendor Offerings	Integrated Solutions Catalogue with Partner Ecosystem	
Lean Assembly Lines	Lean Practices (End-to-End Delivery)	Lean Solutions Factory Competency Centre	Management and Improvement of the Entire Value Stream	Reusable Assembly Lines	Dynamic Allocation and Utilization of Resources
		Processes to Manage Inventory and WIP Limits with Pull System	Regular Improvement Events / Processes (e.g. kaizen)	Leadership 'walking the factory floor'	Supportive Rewards and Recognition System
		Metrics Framework Based on Client Value Creation	Iterative Development	Test-first Delivery	
	Factory Tooling & Automation	Automation of Activities and Visual Controls	Standard Collection of Tooling	Automated Delivery Processes	Integrated Delivery Lifecycle
	Architecture	Embedded Solutions Architects within Delivery Teams	Architects Owning Highly Reusable Components	Dedicated Assembly Lines for Reusable Component Delivery	Reusable Inventory of Solution Components for Product Assembly
Partner Management	Partner Management Capacity	Greater Vendor Management Capacity	Formalized Partnership Engagement	Collaborative Development of Solutions Catalogue	Integrated Cross-Partner Value Streams & Kaizens
	Conversion to COTS Offerings	Increased Analyst Capacity to Map Business Needs to COTS Functionality	Transition from Specialized Developers to System Integration Roles	Curam and Siebel Sustainment Capability	Application of Lean Solutions Factory to Curam and Siebel Delivery
	Efficient Operations & Infrastructure	Effective Partnership with Infrastructure Resources throughout Delivery	Integration of Operations and Service Management into Value Streams	Integration of Infrastructure into Solutions Catalogue	Rapid Provisioning of Environments to Support Delivery

A conceptual value creation network was defined to help the organization visualize how work would flow through the factory and a conceptual enterprise kanban was socialized with leadership to demonstrate the kanban mechanics for the factory.

The factory at 10,000 feet is … a network of interconnected work cells governed by service class policies and work in progress limits to manage capacity

| Ideas are generated and approved using a lightweight process. | Idea realization is analyzed against Cluster capacity and the Solutions Catalogue, and the Business Case is approved if feasible. | The Business Case is assigned to a value stream, further analysis against reference architectures is conducted, and the architecture roadmap is defined. | Initial core team is formed and in-depth model storming is conducted to create the plan and identify assembly lines. | Work is broken up into work items for each assembly line, prioritized for detailed requirements, design, build and test. | Assembly lines coordinate to repackage up work items for integrated release QA and deployment back to the client. |

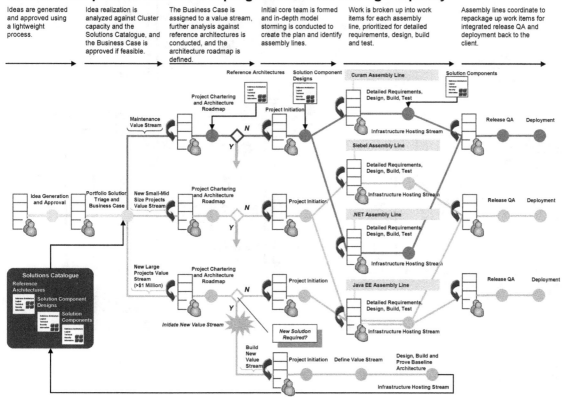

Knowing When to Back Off

In another case it was significantly more difficult to wean our clients off of the specialized, standardized, and commoditized approach to delivery. While working with a separate cluster that was also attempting to redefine itself using a factory metaphor, we found it imperative to soften down the lean/agile rhetoric to a whisper. In this case contradicting the established vision resulted in alienation of executive leadership. Again, trying to find common ground within the factory metaphor was instrumental to moving forward. Fortunately in this case, the definition of a measurable system of work was something that we could agree on.

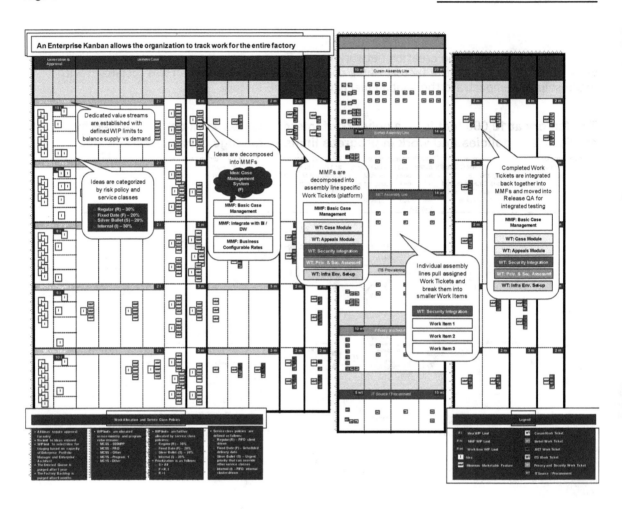

DESIGNING THE SOFTWARE FACTORY

Starting with a Measurable System of Work

Starting with a measurable system of work allowed us to guide our clients on a journey where the destination was much more people- and collaboration-oriented than where they had originally started. The client is now embracing a continuous improvement and quality approach based on Kanban, with Kanban being used on a number of projects with more to come. Rather than attacking the client's perspective on how to improve development head-on, we focused our energies on helping the client design a system of work using components familiar to anybody with Kanban experience.

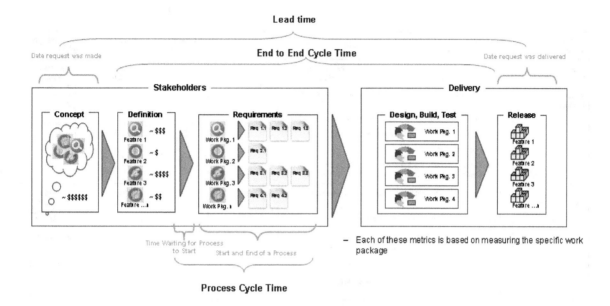

What's a Delivery Factory without Widgets Running through It?

The first step was to convince the client that a factory metaphor lent itself the concept of individual work packages flowing through the system of work in an atomic fashion. Each work package could be categorized according an enterprise collection of work package types, with each work package type representing a unique combination of cost of delay, size, solution, value, and client.

Work Package Types	Description	Prioritization Class	Duration	Cost (Effort * Per diem)	Team Profile
Architecturally Significant Components & Architecturally Significant Use Case	• The exploration, design and build of an architecturally uncertain element (e.g. New Framework, System APIs, Patterns etc.) • Development of enough business functions to validate architecture decisions (Architecturally significant use case sets) • Non-functional and Functional testing to validate Quality, Time, & Effort • Work is tied to a Business Use Case or a System Use Case • High complexity work • 1 Architectural 'concern'. E.g. Service Error Handling with 3-5 explicit requirements with 1 functional process i.e. distinct use case flow	Standard (Medium)	15 Days	35 Days – $26,250	*# of PM: 0.5* *# of BA: 0.25* # of QA: 0.125 # of SD: 0.5 # of Sr. Dev: 1 # of Dev: 1 # Testers: 0.25
JAVA First Release (New Application)	• Enough functionality to justify/enable the business release of a brand new application • Minimal, basic functions (no bells or whistles) • Target subset of users if necessary • Some processes still manual. Minimal error logic • High complexity work • 4-7 Functional Processes i.e. distinct use case flow (Use Case Scenario)	Standard (Medium)	35 Days	90 Days - $68,000	*# of PM: 0.5* *# of BA: 1* # of QA: 0.125 # of SD: 0.5 # of Sr. Dev: 0.5 # of Dev: 3 # of Testers: 1 # Data of Modeler: 0.25
JAVA New Feature for existing application	• A Cohesive set of business valued functionality that is independently designed, built and tested • Extends capability of an application in production or a first release work package • Medium complexity work	Standard (Medium)	15 Days	40 Days – $30,000	*# of PM: 0.5* *# of BA: 1* # of QA: 0.125 # of SD: 0.25 # of Sr. Dev: 0.5 # of Dev: 3 # of Testers: 1 # of Data Modelers: 0.25

We conducted numerous workshops with the entire delivery organization, gathering information about both supply and demand. Demand analysis included demand frequency, budget, and risk profiles. Supply analysis included matching this demand to particular IT groups and technology sets. Work packages were defined and further refined by taking into account large variations in schedule and effort for particular solution sets. We continued to work with our clients to create comprehensive profiles for each work package type, including average effort and schedule, team profile, risk, and of course cost. This allowed us to come up with performance targets, and overall work capacity allocation across the entire enterprise. Finally we took this information and reverse engineered it to get an understanding of the total number of staff to support the delivery factory along with required skill sets. This information allowed the cluster to put appropriate staffing plans in place.

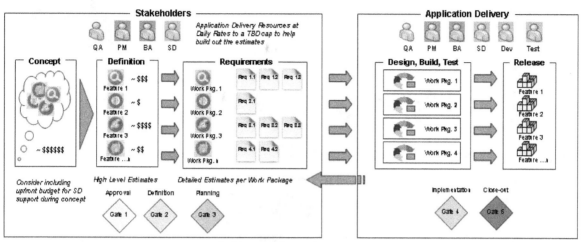

Key Metric – Cycle Time per Work Package

Using Lean Measurements Leads to Lean Delivery

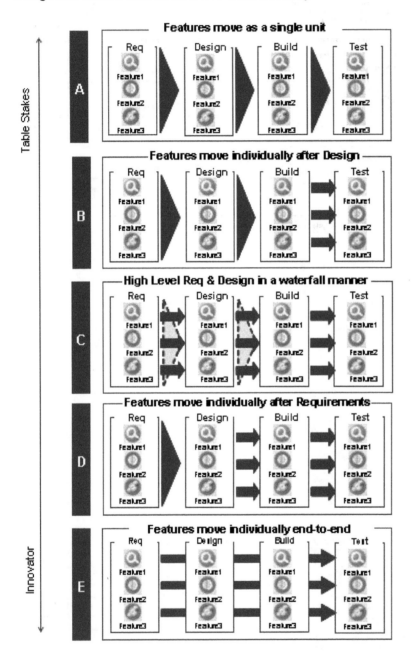

Our client group did not have a preference for more agile approaches to delivery. Rather than arguing the merits of agile over waterfall, we presented our clients with a number of ways that individual work packages could flow through the system. These options ranged from a maximum batch transfer mechanism (e.g. waterfall) to a more single piece flow (e.g. agile). We were able to get agreement that delivery was to be measured according to "factory" metrics familiar to kanban practitioners, including cycle time, lead time, and failure intake. We also helped our client set up a quality management office; we educated the quality specialists on the relationship between inventory and lead time, along with the benefits of cumulative flow diagrams. We also educated these quality specialists on the merits of identifying, analyzing, and removing performance outliers with SPC charts. Using these tools, it became evident to our clients that lower inventory levels would better serve them then higher inventory levels, and that the measurable system of work we put in place for them would actually break down if following a pure waterfall approach.

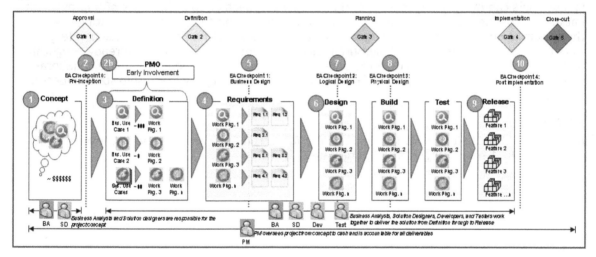

Operationalizing the System of Work - lower k kanban

As the client began to wrestle with how to implement this measurable system of work they asked the obvious question of how to operationalize what they had designed. It was only at this point that kanban was introduced, and only then as an operationalizing enabler, i.e. use kanban to track work packages through your system of work. At this point kanban became very attractive to our clients thanks to the visibility it provided, and the measurable system of work that it enabled. We received permission from our clients to start institutionalizing kanban on a number of projects.

kanban Leads to Kanban

One of the immediate impacts that kanban had on the project was a much deeper understanding of the actual work being completed by everyday staff. Even though kanban was being represented as a work tracking system, its usage allowed for representatives of the client's quality management office to appreciate how work was represented on different projects and how it actually flows through the system of work. It quickly became apparent that much of the upfront design gone into the various work package types across the enterprise was really only of marginal value, especially for domain business problems and technology stack that were not well understood. However, defining the enterprise work packages provided the political capital necessary to execute kanban on a number of projects, which has now resulted in "capital K" Kanban improvement taking place. Moreover, further learning opportunities from the team are being maintained by the centralized quality management group, which is making plans to set up kanban style operational reviews to take place across the entire enterprise.

CONCLUSION

Increasingly, IT is reconsidering how to become a more effective delivery organization. Many organizations are undergoing official IT performance improvement programs. These organizations are often caught between reinstituting familiar command and control oriented paradigm and introducing different approaches espoused by the lean and agile communities. Kanban occupies a compelling value proposition for practitioners trying to help organizations improve. Practitioners can overlay components of the Kanban approach on to either style of improvement initiative to define a potential system of work, and measure performance to evaluating how well the system of improvement is working. Applying the more structured aspects of Kanban (e.g. work package types, metrics, and measurements) to an organization that had already bought in to a top-down, more command oriented approach allowed us to introduce the more collaborative, dynamic, and learning aspects of Kanban without alienating key leadership stakeholders in the process.

REFERENCES

Anderson, J., Hui, A. & Chan A. (2010). *Leaning Towards a Software Factory*. Retrieved 12 February 2011 from http://tempuri.org/page/12

Using Kanban to Achieve Rapid Maturity in Configuration Management

by

Paul Anderson and Dennis Stevens

ABSTRACT

The Kanban Method is a simple scheduling model that can quickly deliver evolutionary maturity to an organization. The model prescribes five core practices: Make Work Visual, Limit Work in Process (WIP), Focus on Flow, Make Process Policies Explicit, and Collaboratively Focus on Improving. To use the model a team can start with what it does now, agree to pursue incremental, evolutionary change, and respect the current process, roles, responsibilities and job titles. As the focus of this presentation we will review how the Kanban Method helped a Configuration Management team that was failing to meet the needs of the business overcome challenges in its environment and achieve a higher level of personal and organizational maturity. The model transformed the team from:

- *Reacting to every customer request to a delivering a predictable cadence based on organizational priority.*

- *Subordination in IT leadership to providing leadership in the IT organization.*

- *Feeling powerless to influencing within and outside their team's processes.*

- *Being perceived as a primary risk to the success of the organization to being a reliable team.*

The Kanban Method is not a silver bullet. However, when followed with discipline, it creates the insight and support necessary for teams and management to understand impediments to flow, recognize opportunities for improvement, and gather insight and supporting data needed to collaborate for improvement across the organization. Using the Kanban Method allows teams to explore options from a fact-based standpoint and explore options for improving the flow of value through the organization.

INTRODUCTION

In October of 2010, a financial services company ("The Bank") was working on a four year project. The technology delivered by this project would provide new functionality, flexibility, and compliance capability to the bank's customers ("Members"). It positioned The Bank for a competitive advantage in an increasingly challenging market. The Bank's leadership viewed this project as critical to the success of The Bank.

This project was leveraging a new architecture and several new technologies for the organization. There were two new large third party products that had been customized to meet specific needs of The Bank. These third party products were connected to multiple existing Member-facing applications through the use of new web services leveraging a new enterprise service bus. These web services also served to integrate third party data feeds. Each of these Member-facing applications had to be customized to interface with the services.

The new architecture led to a need for robust quality assurance (QA) and user acceptance testing (UAT). This became a complicated effort due to the need support multiple baselines. At any time the organization might be testing for current production, the upcoming "Big Release", and multiple upcoming incremental releases. The Bank needed to be able to regression test this integrated application through multiple stages including daily transactions, overnight data consolidation, and month end processing. Since there were significant environmental complexities with this testing, the bank established a Configuration Management team to configure the QA and UAT environments and to stage test data in support of QA and UAT. This team was also responsible for supporting packaging of verified code and any supporting turn-over documentation for production deployment.

Some parts of the organization had been in place for several years – with employees averaging over seven years on the job. There were entrenched methods of development and little collaboration between BA, Development, QA, UAT, and the new configuration management team. The organization had established a formal Software Development Lifecycle that pre-dated the configuration management team.

CHALLENGES

The project suffered from multiple challenges, with a primary focus on the problems associated with the work performed by the Configuration Management team. Around this time, The Bank hired Paul Anderson as the new Director of Information Technology Software Development. There was also a reorganization that involved assigning this team to a manager who had a history of driving difficult change at The Bank. The manager performed an assessment of the Configuration Management Team outcomes and identified specific opportunities to improve the outcomes being delivered by this team.

Delay in QA and UAT was jeopardizing project timelines

The Big Release was imminent and a failed delivery would be harmful to The Bank. The project team identified the Configuration Management team as the single biggest risk to the success of the project. There were constant delays and false starts in QA and UAT caused by problems with configuration. These delays were not only impacting the ability of the organization to test and handle defects from development in a timely fashion, they were also increasing the concern that The Bank would not be able to successfully deploy the application into production. These problems included recurring problems with setting up the rights on databases, getting end-user configured items staged, deployment of the wrong versions of code, and unintended consequences in remote parts of the application.

Failure to get the code staged for production with the right deployment documentation

As the project was progressing, The Bank was subjected to multiple changes in requirements. These led to a need to update production code, the Big Release baseline, and the incremental update baselines. Developers were also working on technical debt and technical improvements that were to be deployed after the Big Release. To support concurrent project efforts, there were various environments, and these required different versions and configuration dependent upon the release schedule relative to "The Big Release". As a result of this complexity, Configuration Management had repeatedly staged the wrong code for deployment to production. Documentation that was to be used by the Engineering (ITE) team was also often inaccurate, resulting in ITE's inability to promote code so that it worked appropriately in production.

Lack of predictability

The low quality delivered by the team resulted in a continuous flow of rework. Combined with the long list of QA and UAT requests, the team was facing increasing pressure on backlog items. This led to the perceived need for the business to expedite requests, raising the demand for more simultaneous testing. Simultaneous testing increased the complexity in the environments that needed to be managed. This became a vicious cycle with decreasing quality and an increase in interruptions to expedited work and resolve issues that were blocking QA and UAT.

Lack of maturity and an inability to improve the situation

To make matters more challenging, the Configuration Management team was relatively new. The members had not developed a mature sense of how to be successful, and the organization's expectations of the Configuration Management role had not evolved toward full development either. The Configuration Management team members were operating from a perception that they couldn't make changes upstream or downstream. They felt an obligation to jump through hoops to overcome upstream quality problems and downstream coordination challenges. They also felt they were operating under compliance constraints that required separation of roles and adherence to a less than mature Software Development Lifecycle (SDLC). The situation resulted in a lack of collaboration and coordination and a lack of a sense of empowerment. The Configuration Management team's response to the perception that it was not performing acceptably was a sense of obligation to react to every customer request on the spot. This created even more complexity, partially completed work, and even poorer outcomes.

SOLUTIONS

The large number of challenges, combined with a lack of maturity in the Configuration Management team and the entrenched position of the various parts of the organization made the risk difficult to address. Paul brought in a consultant who had demonstrated success with addressing these types of challenges in other organizations. The request was to help the team implement best practices to overcome the risks to the Big Release. Upon an initial review of the challenges faced by the organization and the Configuration Management team, the consultant deemed the challenges to be complex problems with interdependent causes rooted across the organization. There was no simple answer to getting the team to implement best practices. Additionally, pressure from the Big Release made it difficult or impossible to address the challenges outside the Configuration Management team directly. An engineered change across the organization was not possible. The consultant worked with the team's manager and they decided to apply Kanban as a method of rapid maturity for the team.

Initial Training

The Configuration Management team went through some basic training on configuration management, establishing and keeping commitments, and the importance of flow in a process. At this point the team members did not feel strongly that this approach was going to improve their ability to meet the needs of the organization. They recognized the need to implement many changes but felt constrained by the organization and a lack of support from other parts of the organization. There was a sense of frustration and resistance to implementing changes into their process when they intuitively understood that much of their problem came from the unreasonable complexity the rest of the organization put upon them. They felt they had tried to fix these problems in the past and that making a change in their organization would just be rejected by the organization.

Make Work Visual

Following the initial training the team established a daily stand-up meeting. In this meeting they listed the work they planned to perform that day, discussed how best to support the work for the day, and reviewed the work completed the previous day. There was a large undifferentiated backlog in the ticketing system. Initially, the team felt it had very little ability to plan the work coming in and were responding to requests as they came in from email.

The team members quickly identified that by understanding upcoming and current testing efforts they could have better foresight into their work and could better support the prioritization of tasks. They added a chart to the wall that showed what testing was scheduled and upcoming in each of the environments. This list became a prioritization trigger for the team. It also highlighted some of the potential conflicts resulting from conflicting demands within testing environments.

Within a few weeks, the team printed all the urgent tasks on a formatted card and placed them on a simple task board. The backlog stretched from the ceiling to the floor. The team members also identified they lacked insight into merging requests into the multiple environments and that there was potential for the lack of visibility to let updates to specific environments slip through the cracks. They updated the ticketing system to highlight what tickets had been applied in the different environments, thus improving their audit capability across environments.

The visibility of testing efforts, combined with the insight gained from the environment specific audits, helped create awareness of testing impacts. This insight helped the configuration team add value to planning and coordination efforts. The Configuration Management team lead started providing this information to the Big Release planning team - providing leadership and value where previously this person had served in a subordinate role. This began to increase the credibility of the team across the organization.

Limit WIP

Listing the work on the wall made it apparent that team members would often have multiple tickets open. This arose from the tendency to drop whatever the team member was doing to jump on the latest crisis from developers, testers, or users. Although no explicit WIP limit was set, the team made the decision to focus on finishing what was started before starting the next task whenever possible. The team was trained on the impact long cycle times had on stalling of work and the impact that high WIP had on complexity in the environments. It became clear to the team how important it was to focus on finishing. Making the work visible and this intentional focus on finishing what was started resulted in a significant reduction in WIP. Reducing WIP also highlighted the impact that complexity from competing demands had on quality and cycle time.

Focus on Flow

Initially, the team focused on two primary metrics to improve flow. The first was First Pass Quality (FPQ). FPQ is a measure of how often a work item arrived, was ready to process, was successfully performed, and met the needs of the business. The second metric was cycle time. Cycle time is a measure of the duration between when an item begins to be worked on until it is delivered.

During the daily standup, the team began reviewing any impediments to first pass quality and its ability to finish what they started the previous day. Basic root cause was done on these impediments and solutions were classified as either internal opportunities or external opportunities. Internal opportunities identify what the team could do to work within the constraints of the organization. The team started acting on its environment to improve its ability to deliver on the expectations of the business. External opportunities identified system imposed constraints. Using the Kanban tracking the team was able to have discussions about the cost of these external constraints. The team was able to negotiate from a data-driven standpoint with parts of the organization outside the team.

Make Process Policies Explicit

The team had operated under a perceived set of constraints - not specific commitments related to quality, time, or their outcomes. Once the team members decided to make process policies explicit, they explored the perceived constraints and made explicit policies for the team (internal opportunities) and negotiated with their upstream and downstream stakeholders (external opportunities) as challenges arose. Making these policies explicit allowed them to explore options for improvement they had not previously considered. It also highlighted the need of the team members to improve the intentionality they applied to their daily work.

Collaboratively Focus on Improving

The information gathered from making the work visible, limiting WIP, focusing on flow, and making process policies explicit identified specific improvement opportunities. Many of these were external opportunities. The team decided to break down barriers while maintaining separation of roles and audit and regulatory compliance. To achieve this they assigned someone from the team to help facilitate upstream and downstream information needs.

IMPACT

Impediment to Flow: Lack of consistent approach

The first internal opportunity impediment to flow involved the team working from memory and not sharing information across the team. This would lead to the team missing steps, resulting in quality problems. Often one team member would perform steps incorrectly when another team member knew the details of how to do the work. Some of this was addressed by reviewing work in the daily standups when individuals shared their approaches, but this was not sufficient. One of the Configuration Management team members had been establishing a directory full of "Things to Know". The team started leveraging the "Things to Know" folder as a shared resource.

Shortly after, the Configuration Management team coordinator began to populate this information into a team Wiki. This helped the team to stop making the same mistakes and increased the rate of growing knowledge across the team. If FPQ items occurred from the same cause, then the team would update the "Things to Know" Wiki. They began to hold each other to a standard of checking the list to ensure they didn't continue to make the same mistakes.

Impediment to Flow: Bad inputs

The first external opportunity impediment to flow was that the turn over documentation and deliverable files they received were not accurate. To improve this, Configuration Management met with Development and collaborated on a solution that would work for both teams. They negotiated an expectation of what "ready for UAT" meant with the delivery teams. They provided a coordinator to help review the turnovers and assist in getting them ready. Then the team implemented a policy that work must be ready before they would start working on it. Since any turnover would eventually be deployed into up to six environments it was important that the documentation got updated and deliverables were properly stored in version control for the initial deployment as well as for the future deployments.

Organizational and Individual Maturity

Over the past 30 years there has been significant work done to measure Organizational maturity. Watts Humphreys' process maturity model found its way into the SEI's Capability Maturity Model. This model is based on types of processes found in organizations. Gerald Weinberg, in Quality Software Management: Volume 1, Systems Thinking (Weinberg, G.M., 1992, Dorset House Publishing, New York, New York), built on Watts Humphreys process maturity models to define organizational management maturity patterns.

Pattern 0-Oblivious:	"We don't even know that we're performing a process."
Pattern 1-Variable:	"We do whatever we feel like at the moment."
Pattern 2-Routine:	"We follow our routines (except when we panic)."
Pattern 3-Steering:	"We choose among our routines by the results they produce."
Pattern 4-Anticipating:	"We establish routines based on our past experience with them."
Pattern 5-Congruent:	"Everyone is involved in improving everything all the time."

Weinberg's Organizational Subculture Management Patterns

Pattern 1-Variable, is marked by heroic individual efforts in unreasonable circumstances. Pattern 2-Routine, is marked by a powerful, controlling manager – leading everyone through force of will. Pattern 3-Steering, is marked by a switch from individual and management heroics focused on delivering the daily work to focusing on management as an organizational development tool.

According to Weinberg less than 15% of organizations make it to Pattern 3. Weinberg finds that the transition to Pattern 3 is difficult because the teams at Pattern 0-2 are overwhelmed and the individual heroics have been rewarded. Additionally, managers lack the desire, training, and experience to successfully function at Pattern 3. However, it is only at Pattern 3 that the organization is a position to sustainably improve beyond the heroic effort of individual contributors and the will of the manager.

Prior to starting with the Kanban Approach, the Configuration Management team leader was struggling to effectively manage the team and coordinate with the rest of the business. They were operating at Pattern 1. The "common sense" solutions of maturing their processes and improving the inputs were not obvious due to the time pressure and complexity that the team operated under. The team members felt they had to respond to the lack of credibility arising from long cycle times and low quality. They tried to regain the confidence of the business by committing to take on even more work and by heroically compensating for the complexity and poor quality inputs that defined their environment. While they were rewarded for their heroic effort, it had become a vicious cycle and the team evolved into the destructive approaches that existed when Paul arrived.

The team members knew they needed to operate differently but felt no power to respond and had no voice in the organization. Their concerns were not considered in the way work was designed at the cross functional level and they were not involved in agreements that were established across teams. Their attempts to communicate their problems were viewed as whining or excuse making. It became commonplace to blame all UAT problems and production problems on "Configuration".

So, the strongest benefit of using the Kanban approach may have been the rapid maturing of the team lead as an effective manager and leader to Pattern 3 management. Kanban helped the team lead gain insight into the system and establish a better understanding of the variation in the system and the impact of this variation on the team. The approach gave the manager courage to act on behalf of the team members supported by data that demonstrated his recommendations would improve performance and the environment. The manager began to seek information outside the team, such as UAT plans and upcoming bug fixes. With this information, the team lead became more proficient in scheduling work for the Configuration Management team. He also began to provide information delivery teams and UAT to help them improve the scheduling of testing and production fixes. This insight helped the Configuration Management team lead establish credibility with other managers. The team lead was able to leverage this credibility, along with data from the performance of the team, in negotiations with the upstream teams to improve performance for everyone. Prior to having the confidence, courage, credibility, and data, the Configuration Management team lead was unable to contribute effectively at this level.

NEXT STEPS

Visibility into the process, clarity gained by limiting WIP, and the focus on flow has identified additional areas for improvement. As the process metrics increase in accuracy, the team will begin to capture upstream and downstream costs associated with cycle time and first pass quality issues. This will be combined with formalized operations reviews, where the team will increase the intentionality of the improvement decisions. They will identify outcomes to measure that ensure changes are delivering the expected results. Additionally, the team will coordinate outside the organization to improve source code management, release management, and continuous integration in support of the improved flow of value. With the new capability of the Configuration Management team, the organization is now ready to establish a release train cadence by extending Kanban upstream from Configuration Management.

CONCLUSION

Within three months of adopting the Kanban model the team had dramatically improved first pass quality, was helping coordinate across the organization, had a clear view of upcoming work, was able to prioritize its efforts to meet the most important needs of the business, and was actively adding capabilities to improve quality and reduce cycle time. The benefits of the Kanban approach allowed an immature team in an entrenched organization to dramatically improve the performance of the team and influence the organization for improved delivery of value. Additionally, the Kanban approach had provided the impetus for the team leader to mature from individual heroics and force of will to using management as a development tool - positioning the team on a path to sustainable and continuous improvement.

From Scrum to Flow at Xbox IT

by

Phillip Cave, Phillip.cave@netobjectives.com

ABSTRACT

The Information Technology organization that supports the E&D division at Microsoft (now known as IEB, the organization supporting the manufacturing and supply chain for Xbox, Kinect, and Zune) had been using Scrum for a few years and had realized that in many cases they were no better off than when they had used large phase delivery. Organization leadership recognized that what was needed was a shift to Lean thinking and flow. They also needed someone to guide a few pilot teams (and eventually the general organization) in the benefits, business drivers, and an approach for implementing Kanban (Lean thinking applied) for the enterprise. This paper is based on my experience guiding said IT organization. Any effort takes internal leadership, so while I was able to provide the outside thought leadership, it really took the inside Microsoft team members to transform the overall organization.

This organization of 300+ people transitioned from a "Scrum on paper but not in execution" model to a highly visible business centric Flow model applying Lean principles (Kanban). Simply put, Scrum was not working for them. This paper will present an entire project and organizational change scenario and will cover the transition from a chaotic "Scrum" model to a model based on Lean thinking, flow of business value, managing WIP, and project buffers. This transition covered changing the execution of business critical initiatives that are implemented with distributed teams (US and India based teams).

INTRODUCTION

The approach began with identifying the natural leadership within what the IEB IT organization calls Solution Managers (think liaison between IT and the business or product owner) and the Program Managers. With a team of execution focused project leaders that grasped the idea of "feature flow", the teams began implementing business value tied to the rhythm of the business. This paper will take the reader through the organizational change and focus on:

1. Defining business value and the consumable feature set.

2. Making all work visible and aligning it to business value.

3. Implementing WIP control using a "crawl, walk, run" rhythm of the business.

DEFINING BUSINESS VALUE

Most existing teams within IEB IT found themselves in a mode of variably ending sprint cycles in order to complete all the work they had signed up for. Two things occurred as these teams neared the end of a sprint cycle (typically we saw about a six week cycle); either there was generally no recognizable business value being delivered, or the sprint cycles were extended multiple times. Either scenario led to frustration from both the business and internal IT leadership. Often these sprint cycles resulted in delivering some technical capability along a technology layer but nothing tangible to which the business could relate. The transformation to a feature flow based model began with showing teams how to break work up into smaller chunks aligned to the business user experiences and business process flows. The teams began to look at work in terms of:

1. What may be consumed by the business quickly.
2. Thinking in terms of business capability instead of technology capability.

Consumable feature set

Since many teams had a practice of continually expanding the sprint scope and/or timelines to beyond two or three months in order to have something to demonstrate to the business, the first focus area was on slicing work along business value. Typically the teams captured business capabilities and scenarios; however, these were not necessarily focused on a tangible user/consumer experience or enabling specific business value.

A key focus area was to show the teams how to break work up into smaller chunks. What resonated well with the delivery team members was communicating along user experience flows and/or business process flows. This approach to breaking work down was paired with negotiating with the business to define the "minimal releasable set" of features to meet the current business objectives. This allowed the business and technology team to realize the pent up value waiting for release, as well as begin to instill confidence and trust within the delivery teams and with the business. This resonated so strongly with one team that it literally stopped its current work to assess what exactly the business was looking to achieve, defined the particular user/business experiences and process flows, and created a release plan based on the near term immediate business value as well as longer term business goals. This team (along with other pilot teams) then began a transformation of defining feature sets aligned to tangible business outcomes upon which to execute in small chunks.

Business Capability

Technology teams sometimes think in terms of delivering a solution based on a functional specification, while forgetting that a functional specification is, in the end, tied to a business requirement definition that essentially defines the capabilities the business needs in order to deliver value to the end consumer. Some technology teams within the IEB organization would align their work along technical capabilities instead of tying their work directly to the business capability. Solutions would be delivered in a disjointed fashion from the business perspective. The technology teams did understand the sequence of work; however, the business was not seeing the tangible value until much later in the delivery cycle.

An example that readers may be able to identify with was used in the organization training that ensued. The business needed the capability to manage its own changes to a customer facing web portal that is based on Microsoft's Sharepoint technology. Essentially the technology team created a content management system with specific capabilities that the business could then consume when assembling new content and pages or modifying the web portal. Think of a "web part" or consumer experience around providing feedback for a particular web experience or web pages — a feedback control. As learning progressed, the business and team recognized that they could achieve business capability in smaller chunks by iterating on a solution. The "feedback webpart" was such a case. The team essentially delivered business capability in two iterations of the solution and first created a basic solution that the business could actually begin using immediately. The team later expanded on the capability based on the current priorities of the business. The experience and recognition that solutions could be arrived at in this manner was the beginning of solidifying a flow based approach to solution delivery.

MAKING WORK VISIBLE

Often the teams, IT management, and business management were frustrated with understanding where their requirements were in the delivery lifecycle, when they would be delivered, how they would know if progress was being met, and how they would know if they were working on the most important things first. In order to answer these questions and give insight into expectations, the organization shifted to expose everything so that the business would understand not only the tangible business value but, just as importantly, the cost of implementing that business value. By everything I mean just that. All features, stories, set up activity, and implementation activity was captured and exposed. Teams are generally comfortable with "features/stories"; however, we introduced "analysis" and "implementation" stories as well to communicate the significant activity that has to occur in order to enable business value. In this sense, work was broken down into business value (features) and enabling business value (set up and implementation activity). This is discussed in the next section.

Given that all the work was exposed, the teams then could start to examine their capacity to perform that work within a defined work flow model. The teams and business could literally see what the work was, what was in process, and where the teams had issues or were stuck. This allowed the teams to focus on the flow of work as the primary measure to progress and allowed them to begin to examine and manage that work that was in process.

Because the teams began making all work visible and measuring progress based on that visibility, a couple of topics naturally played out where the teams began to question the value of activity as measured against delivering the business value. Three such topic areas were:

1. Flow of business value.
2. How much value there is in estimating work that takes days to a week and getting to relative estimates (or no estimates at all).
3. Feature critical chain.

Business Value Flow

The organization shifted to exposing all work and modeling a work flow for that work. Typically the teams captured business capabilities and scenarios; however, these were not necessarily focused on a tangible user/consumer experience or enabling business process. As the teams began to do this, they also began to recognize that they often had work that enabled the business value, and that this too needed to be exposed and tracked. This was seen in the implementation stories mentioned earlier. Given the controlled environment of the larger MSIT organization, there were activities that needed to be done to provision environments, build solution sets, and audit the work among other things. As mentioned, the approach taken was to expose everything so that business would understand what the transaction and coordination costs were to deliver business value in order to make decisions, but mostly to understand effort. Most of the time the business was going to move forward with an initiative and/or feature set, and the IT teams needed to help them understand all the work associated with doing so. It came down to managing expectations. Given that the teams and business could see what the work was, what was in process, what team member was working on what feature/story, and where the teams had issues or were stuck allowed the teams to focus on the flow of work as the primary measure to progress and allowed them to examine and manage in-process work.

To estimate or not to estimate

As teams began to recognize the value of "flow", this thinking had a profound impact on getting team members to grasp "good enough" and the value of learning by doing vs. guessing. Some team members understood that once a team was allowed to "flow", the value of estimating work was zero and work could commence immediately after the business intent was understood. When teams did feel they needed to estimate work or when the business needed a rough idea of the cost of implementing a solution, the teams transitioned from taking days (sometimes over a week) to estimate work down to hours by using a very simple but effective relative estimating exercise used within the agile community.

Before this change in thinking and estimating, teams often used a template to essentially come up with function points for the entire feature set they were asked to deliver within a period of time. The exercise of doing so would sometimes take over a week just to come up with an estimate. This caused a lot of heartburn in the organization. Some teams were measured on how good they could guess how long something would take. Given human nature, teams will feel compelled to spend as much time as they can to come up with an estimate if they are being evaluated on getting their estimates "correct". When the estimate (read: guess) was wrong, as is more often the case than not, this led to more "get the estimate right" behavior, which led to longer cycles to derive an estimate, which led to more frustration. When teams were allowed to pull work and let it flow, the value of spending time to come up with an estimate was replaced with understanding and starting the work. When the business needed to understand its options, the teams created an "analysis story", with the success criteria of the story being to present the options and cost of implementing each option to the business. This analysis story was then turned into a typical business story for later implementation. The behavior shift for some teams was profound and freeing. By spending the time to expose, discuss, and execute, the business and teams began a level of mutually beneficial trust that indeed the right things were worked on at the right time without wasted time to estimate work that was going to be done anyway.

A clarifying note must be placed here. This approach to starting vs. estimating does not mean that teams did not have deadlines or due dates. They did in fact have these. The difference is that conversations ensued to identify which features had a due date and which features did not. In the case of a feature set that had to be delivered by a certain time, by exposing all work and iterating on solutions the business and teams could constantly measure the creation of value as they approached the due date and make decisions weekly about priority, focus, and managing expectations.

Buffers and Critical Chain feature management

Mike Cohn speaks to creating buffers within a critical chain project management aspect (without calling it that) in chapter 17 of his book *Agile Estimating and Planning*. This is an important aspect of any delivery model (Kanban or not) because it helps a team focus on what is most important today.

Critical chain project management (CCPM) may be applied to those projects that fall under special scrutiny and visibility. CCPM, as applied to a business feature driven model, allows a team to monitor a "red/yellow/green" project status using real data on the delivery of features instead of a feeling or gut instinct. Too often I sat in meetings where teams were required to give a color status on certain aspects of a project and the project overall. Time and again I asked what they were basing this "red/yellow/green" status on and posed the question: "What if we based this on the progress of feature delivery against a promised or needed by date?" One particular PM in the organization was well versed with CCPM and began applying a model for the overall PM leadership to use that was based on feature progress against the estimates, the buffer, and the critical path Mike Cohn speaks to in chapter 17 of his book.

As an example of how this was applied, one of the project teams that focused on delivering the user experience around repairing an Xbox had a team discussion that began with this question: *"Do you have to set up your unit test environment or does your unit test environment have to be set up?"* This question was asked because the particular PM understood that the critical path feature at the moment was in jeopardy based on the amount of buffer being consumed due to a stall in progress. The progress was stalled because the engineer in question was working on a task not currently on the critical chain of events (setting up his unit test environment), leading to the detriment of a task on a feature that was on the critical chain of events. Because this question was asked, the response from the team was profound and shifted the thinking from individual team member tasks to a more holistic team approach. The PM on this project understood and communicated to the team the concept of critical chain management and flow of features and tasks. As a result of this team discussion, the team member that was waiting on the engineer to complete a feature task on the critical chain shifted his focus on setting up the engineer's unit test environment so that the engineer could focus on unblocking his team member and make progress against the feature currently on the critical path. The point of this story is that teams have options of using real and tangible data exposed in a feature driven Kanban model to drive the right behavior and focus of the team. This aspect of measuring progress is worth examining and is too detailed for this paper. I encourage readers to explore this and only apply it as needed for their particular needs.

"CRAWL, WALK, RUN"

As the pilot teams began to influence the larger organization, the teams began to be introduced to the concept of "good enough" feature sets along a theme of "crawl, walk, run". This mindset basically poses the approach of getting some business value into the hands of the business now and more value later if desired. This "crawl, walk, run" phrase was introduced by a critical thought leader within the solution management group, Kristin Poole. This led to creating a "standard work/process" with the business to create regular checkpoints that managed business expectations and trust. These "rhythm of the business" checkpoints involved replenishing the business and team queues of work, validating the work, creating a release train, and simplifying the meetings. "Crawl, walk, run" was communicated to help teams understand what good enough for a feature meant, and it was extended into the process execution and thinking along these lines:

1. Establishing a queuing mechanism for the work flow.
2. Creating a business and team rhythm.
3. Changing how teams delivered work.

Business Queue, Team Queue, GO!

A strategy that was developed with teams as they matured in their thinking and execution was to allow the business to solidify on potential features and prepare these in what was termed as the business queue. This business queue was the start of the feature value stream from the business perspective. As long as a feature remained in the business queue the team was insulated from it (they literally had no knowledge of it) until such time as the business was ready to release it to the team for analysis or execution. If the business needed help in understanding the cost of something or needed help in vetting possibilities an analysis story was released to the team. If the business was ready with a definition and success criteria a development feature was released to the team. The analysis or development feature was then placed in the team queue in priority order for the team to pull once capacity was available. The value stream roughly looked like this: Business Queue → Team Queue → Analysis/Vetting → Engineering → Validation → Stage for Release → Released.

The team queue was used as a signaling mechanism that something was ready for analysis or ready for engineering once capacity was available. In this way the solution manager managed both the business driven aspect of the feature set and set the pace for the delivery team, creating both a business and execution rhythm.

Rhythm of the business

An execution rhythm was established over time to manage both business and team expectations. On the business side, the solution manager both vetted new features as well as validated completed features before release to production. In the case where teams were in project/release mode, features were vetted and placed in a "ready for release" queue where they remained until their partner features were also made ready and packed into a release bundle.

This rhythm of the business modified an existing process to drive more frequent information exchanges and management of the delivery value stream. This was done so that the business had clear visibility to feature development as well as defined its responsibility around keeping the flow of features in sync with the rhythm of the team execution. In this way, the business reviewed and made new features available in a just in time fashion.

Team Execution

The maturity of thinking with teams allowed them to begin focusing on completing things in process before starting new things. Before this, some team members on critical high pressure projects were seen working on five or six feature stories at any given time. When this fact was made visible (what was in process and who was touching it), the teams turned the focus to minimizing what was in process and to focus on completing the most critical feature stories faster. This led to significantly minimizing the thrashing (and related stress) of team members.

Another key change was the adoption of a feature flow model where the team members could begin to pull feature stories across the delivery value stream instead of having features pushed at them. As features were made available, team members were allowed to pull work only when they could no longer contribute to something that was already in process. The priority was always to first help unblock work, then finish work in process, and then pull something new into the delivery value stream.

CONCLUSION

It should be noted that while much of this paper focused on getting to a feature flow system, this thinking and execution was put in place while project teams were in the middle of projects where feature sets had to be released in a defined chunk of business capabilities. Once released, some project teams were then allowed to fall into a "sustainment/improvement" cycle of true feature delivery. The point here is that this feature flow approach works well in both project/release based mode as well as a sustainment based mode. The key difference is that in a project mode, features are staged for release, while in sustainment mode features are allowed to be released immediately based on an established agreement with the business.

Think in terms of consumable feature sets. A good approach teams learned was to think in terms of small feature set deliveries based on user experience flows and/or business process flows. This simple yet profound approach really works well in helping teams establish right sized feature stories. Teams had already created "as is/to be" process flows in many instances when they developed their business requirements or functional specifications. The natural tendency was to help teams see that these process flows served them well in breaking the solution problem down into manageable and tangible business centric stories that could easily be fed into the delivery cycle.

Estimate work only if absolutely necessary. Teams typically had taken days to over a week just to estimate work. When this was exposed, teams began to question the value of this (as well as other activities) in favor of actually starting on what they knew today. To be clear, teams still needed to establish a high-level technical and logical architecture to understand the boundaries and domain of their solution set. Once these "roadmaps" were established, teams recognized that nothing was stopping them from picking up the highest priority (critical path) feature and actually working on it. What this meant was teams and management had to work together to remove certain behaviors of being negatively accountable to guessing how long something was going to take and moving forward with rough sizing estimates only when needed. This behavior shift then led to teams being held accountable to focusing on the features in process and removing impediments to progress as able.

Visibility is critical. Only by making all work associated with delivering business value visible can project teams and management make proper decisions based on real data. Teams were able to see the number of things in process, how many items team members were focused on, and the critical chain aspect of features. Because of this exposure, teams and management could then make the proper decisions very quickly based on the knowledge given to them by the exposure of all work.

Establish a rhythm. There is value in understanding expectations and vetting features with the business and teams. A mantra I established with teams was "Time box the activity around the work ... but let the work flow". What this means is allow teams to pull features, but have regular discussions about the features and value stream so that we have clear visibility in what is happening and what we need to do next as an entire team. This means establishing regular intervals or triggers to review work and to maintain the flow of work. We maintain the flow of work by communicating and taking action on impediments as well as ensuring we do not run out of work anywhere in the value stream.

Finally, get out there and experiment. Experiment by first making all work visible. Then take action on what you see. Help teams understand their work from a user experience point of view and deliver that user experience step after step after step. Let teams flow their work but time box decisions around that work. Make decisions as a team based on making all work visible. Deliver in small business driven chunks of work. Have fun doing it!!! ☺

REFERENCES

Cohn, M. (2006). *Agile Estimating and Planning*. Upper Saddle River, NJ: Pearson Education, Inc.

Software Development with Human Values, Powered by Kanban

by

Carlos Churba, carloschurba@gmail.com

Ricardo Colusso, ricardo.colusso@huddle.com.ar

ABSTRACT

Software development is a complex human task. Technology changes, communication challenges, diffuse requirements and scoping, and the inner intangibility of software get combined to increase a project's complexity.

We can apply Kanban to our projects in order to reduce their complexity and mitigate risks. Many articles, papers, books, and research studies confirm the direct benefits of Kanban based on reduced Work in Progress and Teams in "Flow State". However, there is little research or written materials demonstrating how Kanban brings an intense enhancement and appreciation of Human Values among project stakeholders.

In this paper we analyze projects where Kanban has been very effective on fostering Human Values among people and their teams.

INTRODUCTION

The goal of this paper is to share our experience in software development projects in which the use of Kanban powered human values among teams and all project stakeholders.

The adoption of Agile Methods in software development has been a decisive step forward in the industry. After the publication of the Agile Manifesto in 2001, Agile practitioners discovered that, by combining Agile practices with tools and concepts of Lean Manufacturing and Just In Time, it was possible to create high-quality software faster and better. Projects also became more predictable, with teams working "in flow" state, and people were highly motivated. Mary and Tom Poppendiek were pioneers in the application of Lean Manufacturing concepts to software development with their lectures, articles, and books (1).

Kanban is a simple and powerful method to manage Lean software development projects. As Jeff Patton states,

"Kanban development revolves around a visual board we use for managing work in progress. (. . .) The basic idea is stories start on the left side of the board and race across the board through the phases of development they need to go through to be considered "done". Finished stories, ready to release into production pile up at the end. And, because this is a Kanban board and we're going to limit the amount of work in progress, so we'll limit the number of stories we allow on the board. The numbers written on the bottom limit the number of stories allowed at each station." (2)

In the next sections we analyze two software development projects at Huddle Group (3) in which Kanban empowered teams, people, and their Human Values.

CASE 1: BEING AGILE AND FIGHTING UNCERTAINTY IN FRONT OF THE KANBAN BOARD

Huddle Group created a new division for developments in a brand new ERP (Enterprise Resource Planning) platform, assigned a full team to it, and planned a 12-week training program for all members. In week #8 the Huddle Finance department selected a new ERP to streamline its operations, and defined its requirements. Implementation should have been ready four months later, at the time external auditors would inspect all processes in the Finance division. With their planned training still in progress, the team had the option of not taking the project, but in that case the company should have hired a vendor/competitor. So, the team decided to accept the challenge.

Early during its first Planning meeting, the team members found it very difficult to estimate the time and effort of implementing the requests from the Finance division, due to their lack of full technical knowledge of the new ERP development platform.

Considering this issue, team members defined together two possible courses of action:

a) Spend about a month completing their training, making it possible to have more accurate estimations and start implementing the functionality requested.

b) Sort all functionality required by priority, and add the necessary training/research work items as soon as they become critical for doing actual work. Do not estimate time/effort in advance, but rather ensure all backlog items are clearly defined and can be done in less than one day.

Alternative a) was considered by all team members as too risky, since it would have forced them to defer the starting of actual work on the project. On the other hand alternative b) using Kanban would help them to perform valuable work for users from day one.

A few days after the project started, we discovered that Kanban helped the team to stay focused: Every day only the most important tasks — and their related training required for completing them — were discussed and done. Meetings with users were set only if necessary to gather fresh feedback of the new functionality implemented. Very soon we found the team got "in flow state" and was able to achieve the project's goal on time.

Every day team members met in front of the Kanban board to discuss the challenges ahead. From those discussions emerged valuable Attitudes and Human Values such as:

Positive Team Culture and Attitude

The team cultivated a culture with a shared vision to achieve the desired goals. This culture resulted in the creation of positive values shared by team members in front of the Kanban board every day. Team members felt proud and satisfied for helping each other, learning together, achieving technical goals, and growing as persons and professionals.

Communication

Working in a project successfully includes participating in fruitful conversations with a purpose. There is a need for fluid communication so team members can react with flexibility and efficiency to unexpected challenges (4). In this project the team met every day for 20 minutes in front of the Kanban board sharing knowledge, making visible all impediments, and creating new training and research tasks ("*spikes*") on demand. When sharing specific knowledge required more time, separate brown-bag meetings at lunch time were scheduled.

Creativity

Accepting challenges requires courage, and courage is a key characteristic of creative people. In this project team members applied divergent thinking to solve their problems creatively. They also evaluated alternative courses of action in spite of being immersed in uncertainty and anxiety due to their lack of technical knowledge in the new development platform.

CASE 2: IMPLEMENTING NEW FUNCTIONALITY AND CORRECTIVE MAINTENANCE

A foreign customer required services for improving its existing Sales and Marketing system. The requests included corrective maintenance work necessary to adapt the applications to brand new servers and network infrastructure. There was also a demand for new functionality to support new business models.

An initial list of 12 backlog work items was submitted to the team. However, it was expected that new items would be added at any time during the project. All work items were classified as "Urgent", "Important", or "Nice to have". These priorities could also change dynamically.

The four members of the team, who had been trained in Kanban but never applied it in real projects, detected that adopting Kanban to manage the project workload could be a good option to explore, due to the constant changes that were expected in requests and priorities and the need to take care of work items with different priorities.

Team members then discussed how to propose the adoption of Kanban to the customer, trying to anticipate possible issues and concerns. The day after this the team hosted a conference call to inform the customer as to why adopting Kanban could help to balance the workload according to the priorities assigned to the work items. This would be achieved by using Kanban "swim lanes" with different speeds. During the meeting a team member also shared her computer screen remotely with the customer and did a short demo on the electronic tool suggested to support Kanban. Using that tool would enable all project stakeholders to be informed on current work items in progress, work already done, and new work items that would be started next. Additionally, the team would install a webcam in a meeting room to improve communications during remote daily meetings with the customer.

The proposed rules for keeping the team focused and balancing its workload among priorities were:

- Keep a maximum of three Urgent work items in progress at all times.
- Keep a maximum of two Important work items in progress at all times.

- Never have more than one Nice to Have work item in progress.

After 15 minutes of questions and answers, the customer accepted the proposal of adopting Kanban, starting with a one-month test period. After the first month, the team and customer attended a retrospective meeting with the following results:

KEEP	CHANGE
- The team reacted quickly at the time of new Urgent work items, without stopping work in lower-priority ones. - In quiet times with no urgencies there was a significant progress for non-urgent items that had been neglected for months. - It was great for the customer to have full visibility on the work in progress at all times. - Team members liked the variety of work done, including correcting malfunctions and adding new functionality to the system. - Kanban will be adopted for the rest of the project.	- The customer canceled some daily status meetings during week #2. - Some work items were not well defined, so it was not clear when they could become "done". - The team did not communicate in advance to the customer that team members would be out-of-office due to a local National Holiday in week #3.

In this second case we can appreciate the importance of Human Values that guide teams for achieving success in dynamic environments and situations. Among these Values we found:

Empathy

At the time of planning the best way to organize the work, the team considered the expectations and concerns of the customer. The proposal of using Kanban helped the team on one side to limit the work in progress depending on the priority of the items, and on the other side it gave them the chance to empathize with the customer by offering full visibility of the work in progress and better communication through video conferences.

Honesty

The team included the customer in its retrospective meeting, promoting an open space to share experiences and opportunities to improve. Team members were also better able to recognize mistakes.

Responsibility

Kanban helped the team to respond efficiently to the compromise of balancing work on items with different priorities.

Courage

Knowing that using Kanban would enable them to be more efficient and add more value to the customer, the team members decided to go out of their comfort zone and accept the challenge of trying this new methodology.

Integrity

We detected a strong compromise in the team and the customer for delivering on their promises and a positive attitude of helping each other at all times.

CONCLUSION

Processes and tools that guide our projects have a strong effect not only on the results achieved, but also on all project stakeholders. Selecting and mastering agile methods and keeping our teams guided by Human Values makes it possible to achieve high levels of sustainable motivation and productivity in complex software development projects.

ABOUT THE AUTHORS

Carlos Churba is a psychologist and architect, Chief Professor of Creativity and Innovation at Universidad de Belgrano (Buenos Aires, Argentina), researcher, and lecturer on how to make people and teams more creative and effective.

Ricardo Colusso is an Agile Manager at Huddle Group and Professor of Creativity and Innovation at Universidad de Belgrano.

REFERENCES

(1) See Lean Software Development: An Agile Toolkit (2003) by Mary and Tom Poppendieck

(2) Fragment from Jeff Patton´s Agile Product Design blog article, http://www.agileproductdesign.com/blog/2009/kanban_over_simplified.html

(3) Huddle Group is a Software Development Company based in Argentina, with customers in the United States, Europe and Latin America http://www.huddle.com.ar

(4) Fragment from Carlos Churba's Crealogar blog http://crealogar.blogspot.com

Outside-In Risk Management

by

Julian Everett, julian.everett@gmail.com

ABSTRACT

This paper describes a systems thinking approach to risk management that has been recently developed within a business-to-consumer digital media organisation. The approach treats product development as a speculative investment activity, and uses risk-adjusted valuation of feature set proposals as a tool for guiding decisions regarding what to implement and when. Through an exploration of product diffusion, market risk, and various sources of internal risk, it sets out a customer-driven model for increasing the reliability of return on technology investment. A discussion of the challenges of embedding the technique into business delivery teams is also included.

INTRODUCTION

The ability of an organisation to generate reliable return on its technology investment depends on its capability to perform effective risk management. This paper describes a risk management approach that has been recently developed within a business-to-consumer digital media organisation.

WHAT IS RISK?

In the simplest terms, risk is the probability of an undesirable outcome. For technology investments, the intended outcome is the generation of business value. Business value is a complex concept that reflects the aggregated values and goals of stakeholders; however, for any commercial organisation it is rooted in financial viability. Financial viability is achieved and sustained by performing the following, in alignment with core commercial strategy:

1)   Revenue generation

2)   Revenue protection

3)   Cost savings

Each of these will have associated risks. For example:

1)   Revenue generation: Is the market ready? Might a competitor launch before me?

2)   Revenue protection: Is the stream really protected? Is its cost now prohibitive?

3)   Cost savings: Are there hidden costs I have not considered?

Basic financial viability is of greatest concern prior to product launch and again prior to product retirement. Between these points, once profitability has been established, higher strategic goals often take precedence. For example, an organisation might focus on editorial excellence or building collaborative partnerships with a few key customers over unbridled growth. Risk management of higher-level goals can be conducted on top of the continued management of financial viability using the same principles that are described in this paper. However, in the interests of simplicity, the scope of this discussion will be limited to economic concerns.

THE BUSINESS VALUE DELIVERY CYCLE

For any organisation that has adopted test-driven agile delivery practices such as BDD, a systems view of its technology investment cycle can be represented as follows:

Figure 1. The Business Value Delivery Cycle

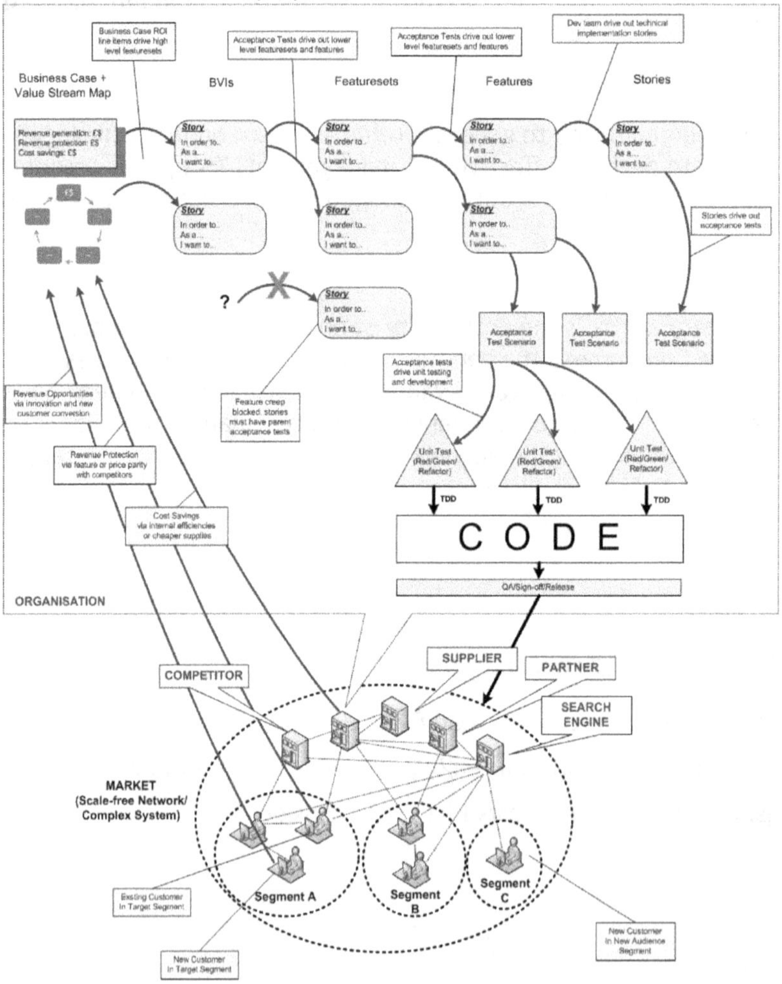

It is a pull process, driven by the needs of both existing and potential new customers in the complex ecosystem of the marketplace. This perspective shifts the dividing line between requirements and solution upstream. It treats product development, marketing, user experience, and technology as subcategories of solution delivery, and emphasises the collaborative nature of value generation within any organisation.

Figure 2. Business Requirements and Solutions

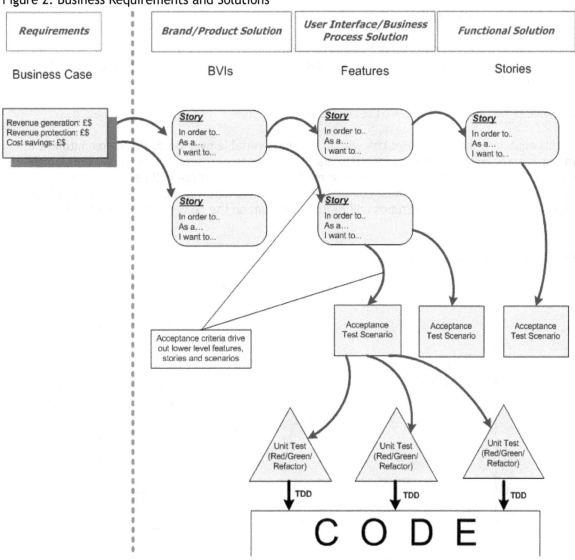

A SIMPLE VALUATION MODEL

The return on investing in any solution is only guaranteed once it is actually realised. Prior to that, the value will be a function of its probability (where all values are estimates or forecasts):

```
Current Benefit Value = Probability of Realisation x Business Value
```

The probability of realisation will be directly dependent on risk:

```
Probability of Realisation = (1 - Cumulative Risk)
```

In contrast to benefits, costs do not need risk adjustment; once they have been incurred they are sunk. This gives us a starting point for thinking about risk-adjusted valuations of any investment proposal:

```
Estimated Value = ((1 - Cumulative Risk) x Forecast Value) - Estimated Cost
```

In this equation, the cumulative risk will be the main variable over time. If the commitment to invest is made too early before adequate analysis has been performed, then it will entail high levels of uncertainty. If the commitment is made too late then there will be an increasing risk of delayed delivery. As a result, most cumulative risk profiles follow some kind of skewed "U" curve. The optimal point to commit funds will be the minimum on the "U", or at the point of highest risk-adjusted valuation.

Figure 3. The Optimal Exercise Point

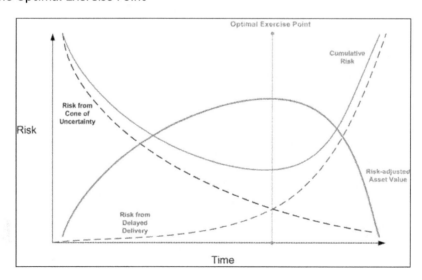

It is worth noting that delay is treated as risk rather than cost. This is because cost of delay is hard to model in volatile markets like digital media. For new product innovations, the cost of delay might be very little as long as first-mover advantage is maintained. Should that be lost, however, then the cost will suddenly spike. The spike point is exceptionally difficult to predict, and so estimation of the associated cost at any given time is equally difficult. It is easier to treat the spike simply as an event of increasing probability over time.

It should be strongly emphasised that the aim of this model is not accurate risk-adjusted pricings. Many risks will have probabilities in the same or lower range than the error margins in both the model and the input data, making the exact result of estimation calculations of little value. The core aim of a commercial risk model should instead be simply to increase the likelihood of organisation survival by the enhancement of its decision making capabilities (Jorion & Taleb, 1997). To that end, effective risk management is primarily concerned with risk identification and mitigation rather than pricing.

The model is useful instead for the following reasons. Firstly, it provides a general description of risk distribution over time. Secondly, it creates a common framework for thinking about all types of risk that emphasise:

1)   Technology investment should be performed in a highly incremental manner in order to spread risk;

2)   Funding should only be committed after an initial phase of risk analysis;

3)   Risk should be managed and prioritised as a function of the value from which it derives.

Thirdly, the act of performing the analysis can capture additional, very valuable information and insight.

RISK IDENTIFICATION

The most difficult aspect of risk management is risk identification. If the identification process is performed poorly, then risks will be missed and a misleading sense of confidence will be created. Closed-loop value stream maps are a useful tool in this respect. They give a product-centric systems perspective of the complete end-to-end value generation process. An example for an ad-funded digital media business-to-consumer product might be as follows:

Figure 4. An example closed-loop value stream map

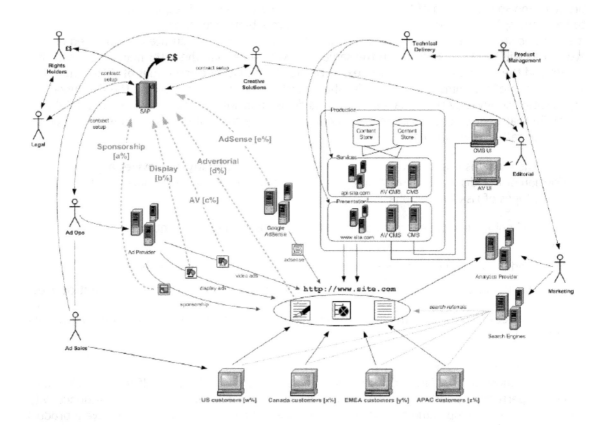

The map should include every step within which risk could be introduced into the system. Each step in turn then needs to be analysed for all categories of risk relevant to the line of business. For digital media organisations, the following category headings have proved useful.

1. Market Risk

Much of the most influential marketing analysis of the last 10 years (Godin, 2001; Gladwell, 2002) has highlighted the viral nature of product growth. Markets behave as scale-free networks that contain a long tail of very high connectivity nodes, and these hub nodes act as product diffusion gateways into the various demographics, or sub-nets, which comprise the marketplace. The mechanisms involved are essentially the same as those that determine the spread of infectious disease.

These ideas are based on meme theory, which was first formulated in "The Selfish Gene" (Dawkins, 1976). A meme is a unit of cultural information; for example, a product feature (which gets expressed as an artefact in the world): source code, graphic design, or advertising, and that artefact then influences the chances of the meme being replicated — i.e. the product growing in the market. This is the key to understanding market risk. Any business idea that might generate revenue, protect revenue, or save costs — in short, any Business Value Increment — is, in essence, a meme competing in the complex system of communication and interaction that defines a marketplace.

This explains the problem of forecasting long term return on investment (ROI) from technology product development. Over a period of years, ROI will critically depend on the unpredictable success or failure of a product to "tip over" and diffuse through the few hub nodes that open up whole new market segments.

The only way to manage market risk reliably is via a highly incremental investment and growth model. By decomposing the complexity into an ongoing sequence of simple, small, and short-term investment decisions, the total risk exposure at any moment is minimised.

2. Commercial Risk

A first subcategory of commercial risk is legal risk. For a digital media organisation, this covers rights management, libel, data protection, and PCI compliance obligations. A second category includes activities that are fully legal, but create reputational risk by undermining the organisation's core strategic values. An example might be the publication of factual inaccuracies which undermine editorial credibility.

Revenue forecast uncertainty is another common source of commercial risk. That uncertainty might be due to a number of factors that can be mitigated to varying degrees, including the intrinsic volatility of the market, a lack of market analysis, or a poorly crafted or incomplete financial model.

Finally, accounting risk can create problems capable of crippling an organisation. This occurs when the profit and loss reporting lines do not reflect the real flow of value through the organisation. This results in misleading assessments of financial viability. For example, a cross platform publishing strategy might use the web for raising brand awareness in order to attract more TV viewers and generate increased TV ad revenue. However, if the P & L accounts are structured on a per platform basis, then web product increments will always appear to be non-viable, which will then block the growth of TV ad revenue.

3. Operational Risk

Operational risk covers effective application and service level monitoring, alerting and escalation procedures, support functions, and editorial and technical maintenance. Typically such concerns are among the most frequently expected and identified delivery risks.

4. Usability Risk

The success of any human interfaced product will depend on good user experience design. It might be both a technically excellent and commercially robust product proposition, but without an elegant user interface, consistent and easily comprehensible visual language, a compelling, unobtrusive graphical design, and continual user testing customers are highly likely to choose other, more user-friendly competitor products.

5. Technical Risk

Technical risk covers non-functional requirements such as security, scalability, performance, reliability, exception handling, and redundancy. It also includes the use of new languages, tools, libraries and services, deviation from public standards, too much or too little upfront design, and all avoidable architectural complexity. These subcategories are all related to product delivery.

A second group of technical risks relate to the longer term total cost of product ownership. These include but are not limited to: code quality, testability, test coverage, coupling, and cohesion, and the quantity, direction, and stability of dependencies — all of which fundamentally impact the speed and cost of software change. The more volatile the domain, the greater the susceptibility of an organisation to these risks. As a result, for digital media organisations operating in highly dynamic marketplaces, such concerns are — or should be — critically important.

6. Cognitive Risk

Cognitive risks are associated with the decision making process itself. At the most basic level is an unjustified belief in "gut-feel" or intuitive decision making, where the quantity of correct decisions is statistically no better than random. This is often coupled with cognitive biases, which leads people to minimise or discount refuting evidence.

Once the need for analysis has been recognised, the next type of risk is associated with the model itself. The aim of risk modelling is to create the simplest possible tool that all stakeholders understand and that steers them to make correct decisions when the impact of failure is greatest. For this reason, unlike other forms of domain modelling, it is not concerned with high accuracy representations of the world. Additional model complexity should only ever be introduced when over-simplification is itself creating risk of wrong decisions being made. This is because adding complexity also adds the risk that stakeholders may no longer understand how the model works. This is exacerbated when using spreadsheets, where the error margins in both the assumptions and input data are hidden and the outputs are expressed to a misleadingly large and meaningless number of decimal places. Any such "black box" tools have grave disadvantages in that they hide large amounts of highly valuable information and block the possibility for continual improvement of risk management practice. For these reasons, risk models should be self-reflexive; they should make visible the risks entailed by the modelling process itself.

Data-driven decision making can also be a source of risk. Firstly, if data is used from past contexts that are dissimilar to the present in any significant way, then it will lead to false conclusions. Secondly the data set may have low domain coverage, and so the lack of an event occurring in the past will be no guarantee against it occurring in the future. Thirdly, there is the risk of confusing statistical correlation with causation. For example, correlation between adoption of some new programming practice and reduced bug counts may be simply due to the above average coding skills of the early adopters rather than the programming practice.

Data-related risks are particularly dangerous as they create the illusion that due diligence has been performed. A general principle of risk management is that no knowledge is better than false knowledge; in the former circumstance, stakeholders are at least aware of the fact that they know nothing.

RISK MITIGATION

Once risk identification has been performed, the next step is the mitigation of all risks that can be cost-effectively removed.

Figure 5. Risk Mitigation

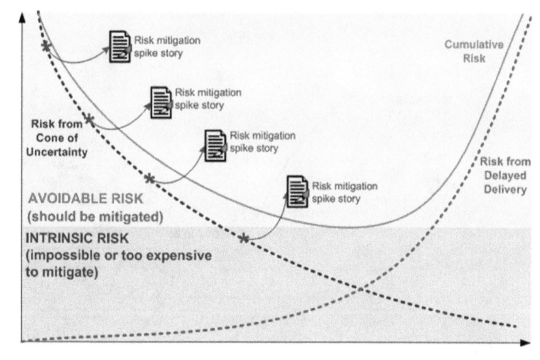

All non-trivial risks should be addressed, and so assessments of probability and impact are not a critical dependency. They are mostly of use for prioritisation so that any large inherent risks are flushed out as soon as possible before further costs are incurred. The concepts of probability and impact are of more help in terms of mitigation strategy. Options include:

1)   Decrease risk probability (if possible, to zero).

2)   Decrease risk impact (if possible, to zero), either directly or indirectly via insurance policies or the creation of fallback options.

3)   Decrease both impact and probability.

4)   Accept risk when mitigation is either too expensive or not possible.

If the levels of intrinsic risk are unpalatable to stakeholders, other solution options should then be explored.

Figure 6. BVI Solution Options and Risk Mitigation Story Tree

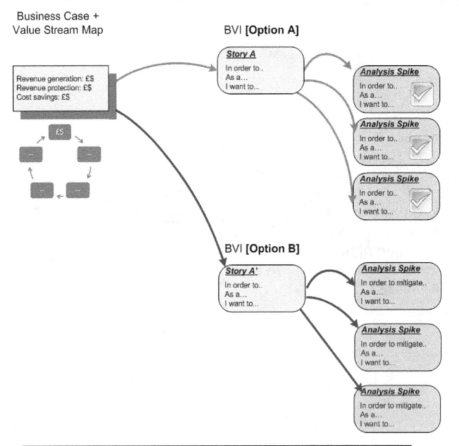

A two-tier product management kanban board is an excellent tool for facilitating this. It has a swim lane for each market opportunity, which spawns one or more BVI exploitation options and a collection of risk mitigation stories for each BVI. Each risk story is then pulled through queues for specification (where stakeholders agree mitigation acceptance criteria), mitigation, and sign-off, at the end of which product managers decide whether to commit funds to implementation or not. For BVI options that they do decide to exercise, the relevant card is then pulled into the first buffer of the technical delivery board. This is described in the diagram below.

Figure 7. Product management two tier kanban board

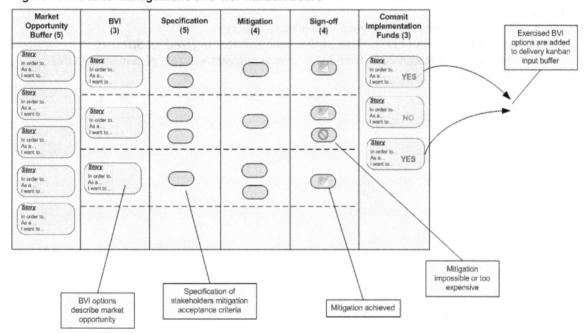

ADOPTION CONSIDERATIONS AND CONCLUSION

This technique can be very effective, but seeding its adoption is sometimes challenging. It quite powerfully undermines the service provision model of technology delivery and the illusory separation between "the business" and IT departments. Greater shared responsibility for value generation and much closer collaboration across business functions is promoted as a result. Initially this can be uncomfortable. Delivery management might feel insecure as traditional definitions of the success for which they are accountable become less relevant. Analysts, testers, and architects will be prompted to ask probing questions about the business case, financial models, and reliability of forecasts, which can be intimidating. Equally, such questions can be misconstrued by product management and finance as threatening.

For these reasons, the approach works best in situations where there is already a high level of trust and collaboration between the delivery team and other stakeholders. In such receptive circumstances, it can foster new levels of communication and teamwork, where business analysts pair with finance, architects pair with product managers, editors pair with marketing and sales, and all within an environment of greatly heightened risk awareness. The results of working in this way can substantially transform the long term value generated by a business division.

REFERENCES

Dawkins, Richard (1976). The Selfish Gene. New York, NY: Oxford University Press.

Gladwell, Malcolm (2002). The Tipping Point: How Little Things Can Make A Big Difference. Boston: Little, Brown.

Godin, Seth (2001). Unleashing the Ideavirus. New York: Hyperion.

Jorian, Philippe & Taleb, Nassim (1997). The Jorian-Taleb Debate. Derivatives Strategy Magazine. Retrieved 11 March 2011 from http://www.derivativesstrategy.com/magazine/archive/1997/0497fea2.asp

Leaner Programmer Anarchy

by

Fred George, fredgeorge@acm.org

Antonio Torreno, antonio.torreno@forward.co.uk

ABSTRACT

At Forward Internet Group in London, we are practicing a post-Agile style that follows few of the *standard Agile practices. Yet the style conforms to the Agile Manifesto (Beck, 2001) and the XP Values (Beck, 2005) ascribed by Kent Beck. We call this style Programmer Anarchy. This style is not unique with us; indeed, we know other firms (including financial trading firms) who follow this style, as well as the Facebook development team (North, 2011).*

Much as the movement from waterfall processes to Agile has shifted roles and titles, we have seen additional shifts in roles and titles when moving from Agile to Programmer Anarchy. Similarly in this shift, we have seen benefits in even faster delivery to market, improved team morale, and market-correct functionality.

This paper characterizes the new environment of Programmer Anarchy, examines the significant Agile practices that have been rendered moot with Programmer Anarchy, and closes with a discussion of the aspects at Forward that have enabled Programmer Anarchy.

EVOLVING TRUST RELATIONSHIPS

In the beginning...

Traditional (waterfall) processes are characterized by requirements specifications by customers being passed to developers to implement. In this contract between the parties, the roles and responsibilities are clear. The waterfall processes allow for separation in time and location between the parties; indeed, the oft-cited benefit of complete specification is to be able to outsource the implementation to lower cost labor. Failure rates are high, and are little helped by process tools. Rather, the tools in the last 20 years have only helped to properly assess blame for the failures, rather than preventing failures. Such is the purpose of contracts in general.

Trust between the parties is not assumed. Indeed, we would argue that trust has diminished over time, partly due to outsourcing arrangements, but at least equally due to the increased complexity of the applications under development and the increased economic pressure to deliver more quickly in a rapidly evolving marketplace.

Agile effect on trust

Agile seeks to establish a more equal partnership between the customer and the developer. Conversations between the parties are encouraged (whether Scrum's sprints, daily stand-up meetings, or XP's on-site customer practice). As consultants we have seen trust reestablished between stakeholders and development during the first Agile projects in an organization.

But the renewed trust has not come easy. "Trust me," has been said too many times with too few successes. Skepticism reigns. We have found that the skepticism is usually overcome by great desperation, desperation usually brought on by the combination of a critical business need and a failing traditional plan. However, once established, the organization delights in the new trust relationship, and the trust grows steadily from delivery to delivery. The transition is accompanied by several ancillary traits:

- The need for detailed specifications diminishes to the point of vanishing.
- Jobs become roles, with most individuals able to play several roles.
- The importance of job titles wanes.
- Teams in place solely to coordinate (*project offices*, for example) become redundant.

These factors among others create a social cost to the organization to transition from traditional to Agile methods. It is not a smooth, continuous process from traditional to Agile, but rather more of a revolution, a discontinuity: jobs disappear, titles become less important, power shifts. Mark Durrand of uSwitch first labeled this gap or cultural chasm to be overcome when an organization shifts from traditional methods and Agile methods (Durrand, 2011).

On to Anarchy

A shift to Programmer Anarchy creates yet another cultural chasm in the organization. Once again, we have seen roles redefined and certain jobs disappear. And as for trust, even more is required between the stakeholder and the developer.

CHARACTERIZING PROGRAMMER ANARCHY

Programmer Anarchy exhibits three distinct differences from Agile methods, but also shares one key characteristic.

Reduction in roles

The term Programmer Anarchy derives from the reduction in roles. Gone are the roles of Business Analyst, Quality Assurance (or Tester), and Project Manager. The only remaining roles are Stakeholder (or Customer, which we will use interchangeably), and Developer. In our environment at Forward, there are not even Managers of Programmers.

So how can such a group function? Through the classic concept of *anarchy*, defined as the simple absence of publicly recognized government or enforced political authority. We want to let the programmers as a social group organize and reorganize themselves as they see fit.

The missing roles become unnecessary for different reasons.

Business Analysts serve to understand the needs of the Customer, and to translate those needs for consumption by the Programmers. In Agile, the unit of consumption is a *story* (Beck, 2005). We would contend that from a perspective of value, no business value is created by transferring knowledge into the head of a Business Analyst, who then must convey that knowledge into the head of a Programmer. There is potential for information lost in the double-exchange. At a minimum, time is lost in this double-exchange. And all this is compounded if a Developer has a question for the Stakeholder that has not been anticipated by the Business Analyst. In our experiences as consultants, we cannot recall an engagement where, as a Developer, we have not become one of the top Business Analysts for an enterprise simply because we have implemented a complex portion of the business for the Stakeholder. So, at Forward, we have never had the middleman of a Business Analyst between the Stakeholder and the Developer.

Nor has Forward ever employed anyone in Quality Assurance. First, having someone dedicated to that role creates yet another person that needs knowledge transfer in order to be effective. Second, the architectures of our systems have generally rendered QA moot, with the pieces of the system being ridiculously simple, and the overall system being sophisticated enough to require architectural skills to comprehend (no sweet spot for a traditionally trained QA role). Third, we have shifted to active monitoring of our systems, an activity very akin to pre-deployment acceptance tests. With the myriad of external services which our systems use, monitoring provides the needed robustness with the inevitable failures (whether ours or an external service), and is a much more valuable asset to create than acceptance tests.

The demise of Project Managers arises out of answering some questions of ourselves. Among the roles of Stakeholder, Manager, and Developer, who is best qualified to:

- Decide how much effort is required on a certain project? We answer: Developers.
- Determine the best team to assign to a project? We answer: Developers.
- Decide when a Developer can afford to roll off a project? We answer: Developers.
- Decide the priority among projects in the face of scarce resources or time? We answer: Stakeholders.
- Guide a Developer in career growth? We answer: Other Developers.

As you can see, we don't answer "Manager" for any of these questions.

Missing Agile practices

As we have discussed Programmer Anarchy with colleagues and groups, the most astounding reactions occur when we list the Agile best practices we don't follow:

- Stand-ups
- Story narratives
- Retrospectives
- Estimates (of stories)
- Iterations
- Mandatory pairing
- Acceptance tests
- Unit tests
- Refactoring

- Patterns
- Continuous integration

As you can see, the list is long and full of accepted, "required" practices. Let's discuss the reasons that these have fallen away.

Our developers trust one another, and have mutual respect for the opinions of each other. Developers working on the same project sit in close proximity to each other (the same table, generally as close as possible). *Stand-ups* to check on the status are unnecessary; everyone knows what is going on. *Story narratives* are unnecessary as developers will talk about what is needed continuously, without the burden of writing it down in detail, or worse, having someone approve it. Trust and mutual respect eliminate the need for *retrospectives*; they feel comfortable questioning process and adopting/discarding ideas freely. Trust and mutual respect also renders *mandatory pairing* unnecessary; a Developer is comfortable enough with his colleagues to ask for help when needed, or to assist his colleagues if they are stuck.

With their focus on the business (wrought by eliminating the Business Analyst barrier between them and the Stakeholder), they use business metrics as the measures of success. The focus is on results, not on creating fear to innovate. *Estimates* beg to be compared to actuals; that leads to more pointless discussion about why there was a difference between estimates and actuals (something that a Manager role can really get sink his teeth into). So don't make estimates; rather focus on doing what is most important, and if it is too hard, do something else. With that attitude, *iterations* lose all value.

Forward has embraced services architectures, and strives to build simple services deployed in frameworks. Developers focus on keeping each micro-service small, often having it do only one thing. If the need to enhance the service arises, the service is simply rewritten. It is a rare service that doesn't need changing on occasion, so no service is actually very old. If services are small and have short life spans, there is a set of best practices (designed to create maintainable, long-lived applications) that are rendered moot: *acceptance tests, unit tests, refactoring, and patterns.*

Finally, we practice *continuous deployment* of the small applications in lieu of *continuous integration* of a bigger application. Statistics bare this out: From active monitoring of GitHub over a recent seven day period, 38 of our developers deployed 492 times against 86 projects. That is a pace of one deployment every five minutes of a business day. Rather than focus on perfect deployments (although it is harder to make mistakes on something small), we focus on rapid rollback and staged deployments to catch the inevitable slips. We note that this is consistent with the Lean tradeoff of *fast failure* over *defect prevention*.

This continuous deployment is worth one more footnote on roles. Developers do their own deployments, mostly into virtual machines in the cloud. Much of the traditional IT role of controlling the deployment environment has disappeared. It makes us faster.

New, broader trust relationship
We initially discussed the shift in trust required in moving from traditional processes to Agile processes. The move from Agile to Programmer Anarchy requires a similar shift in trust.

In our environment at Forward, Stakeholders set goals and objectives to be accomplished and leave the implementation of those goals and objectives to the Developers. The Stakeholders may be constantly consulted for domain knowledge, but they are no longer the source for stories, nor are they setting the priority of stories day to day. The Stakeholders *trust* that the Developers will drive to meet the goals and objectives in the most clever, efficient way.

We avoid the trap we are now calling *Story Tyranny*. Consider the following environment:

- Development is driven through stories;
- Stories are small;
- Customer/Stakeholder sets the priority of stories; and
- Estimates, metrics, and deliverables are centered around stories.

It sounds perfectly Agile, and it is. We had teams in this environment, yet we found our Developers were becoming unmotivated, focusing solely on delivering the stream of stories they were presented as fast as possible. Their understanding of the business environment they were building was unexploited. Time to reflect on the direction and suggest innovative changes was missing. In essence, they had become mindless drones to the story process.

With Programming Anarchy running successfully in other parts of the organization, it took very little to shake the developers out of their lethargy. "What do you think we should be doing? Why aren't you doing that already?" Now they are doing the things they think will make the project successful, and organizing themselves around the task the way they think is best. Anarchy in action. Stakeholder trust.

Common Traits Between Agile and Anarchy

In one way, we would be hard pressed to argue that Anarchy is not another form of Agile. Reviewing each of the elements of the Agile Manifesto (Beck, 2001), we concur with them all. Reviewing each of the XP values (feedback, communication, simplicity, courage, and respect) (Beck, 2005]) we equally subscribe to these. Indeed, if anything, we could claim we have more feedback, rely on greater communication, create even simpler solutions, and so on. That is hardly a difference.

At the end of the day, however, the reduction of roles, the myriad of missing Agile standard practices, and the new level of trust required between Stakeholder and Developer lead us to conclude that Programmer Anarchy is indeed post-Agile.

ENVIRONMENTAL ENABLERS

We acknowledge that at Forward, we have some environmental elements that contribute directly to the success we are enjoying with Programmer Anarchy.

Business environment

Forward, founded six years ago, focused on Internet advertising in its early years. In this cowboy environment, bets were placed on search terms in vicious bidding wars. Financial success meant finding the 90% losing search terms quickly, and cutting those losses, while focusing the 10% successes on compound growth. Thus our founder, Neil Hutchinson, was rewarded for being risk-affine (in contrast to risk averse). Our culture is rooted in taking chances, accepting lots of failures, finding failures quickly, and capitalizing on our successes. Failures are not over-analyzed; that wastes a lot of time. Similarly, successes are not over-analyzed either. We just accept them and exploit them.

Forward has enjoyed years of triple-digit growth under this philosophy. Financial success in combination with our risk-affine nature encourages (and even demands) constant experimentation that we undertake every day.

Developer culture

About four years ago, Forward brought in ThoughtWorks to implement a new commercial Web site. ThoughtWorks over-delivered in a short, 10-week project. Neil Hutchinson and his team recognized two things: Agile processes are brutally efficient and remarkably predictable, and fewer skilled programmers armed with supporting tools and processes are more valuable than large numbers of outsourced developers. Over the next year, Forward began recruiting skilled (and relatively expensive) developers, turning them loose on various projects. Financial results grew quickly.

Neil seeded a programmer into a key revenue-producing group that had just lost its manager. Left to his own devices, this programmer built what he needed to get his job done and support the rest of the team. They made more money. He did additional things on his own initiative. More money again. Not one to miss the obvious, Neil pushed more skilled programmers into the mix with even greater benefits accruing. Thus began Programmer Anarchy.

The programmers exhibited several key characteristics. In general, they had broad industry experience from consulting, derived personal satisfaction from delivering software that others really use, and a thirst for more technical knowledge. They respected each other, and invited others to join them only if they felt mutual respect would be preserved (our recruiting process aligns with this in the obvious ways).

In summary, Forward is developer-focused, our developers have clarity of business success, and respect one another.

Experimentation drives innovation

Our developers identified a core belief themselves: *Experimentation drives innovation.* Often experiments fail; the experiments of our developers are no different. Their first attempt to do something with map-reduce failed, and ditto for their first use of Clojure as an alternative to our default Ruby preference. Nevertheless, the developers learned. These learnings were soon applied to new problems for which these technologies did work. Our production Hadoop cluster runs thousands of jobs for us daily, taking hours instead of days to do the work we require. Clojure is now at the heart of several of our systems, exploited for what it does best.

Courage, aka fearless

We believe that fear kills the spirit of the individual and the team, is a powerful de-motivator, and frankly makes work feel like work. Forward continually strives to eliminate fear through its practices. If we want to be truly successful, we cannot let fear tame us. Paul Fisher, one of our new senior leaders with a VC background, wrapped up his first presentation to the company by quoting, "The greatest barrier to success is the fear of failure." (Eriksson)

From the top of the company on down, we work to keep fears at bay.

Required environmental factors

The environmental factors we have discussed above are certainly sufficient to enable Programmer Anarchy. We can't say with any certainty, however, that you need all of them in order for Programmer Anarchy to succeed. Indeed, we hope that you would need far fewer of them for success. For us, this is an area of interest and further study.

CONCLUSION

Programmer Anarchy represents an evolving set of practices that offers an alternative to Agile practices. The successful adoption of Programmer Anarchy in Forward and a few other companies bodes well. Still, it seems premature to announce the demise of Agile without more adopters as well as more experience with the execution of Programmer Anarchy.

REFERENCES

Beck, Kent, et al (2001). *Agile Manifesto*. Retrieved 18 March 2011 from
http://agilemanifesto.org/

Beck, Kent (2005). *Extreme Programming Explained, 2nd Edition*. Retrieved 18 March 2011 from
http://www.physicsdaily.com/physics/Extreme_programming

Durrand, Mark (2011). *Personal conversations in February 2011.*

North, Dan (2011). *From months to minutes – upping the stakes.* QCon London 2011.
Retrieved 18 March 2011 from http://qconlondon.com/london-2011/presentation/
From+months+to+minutes+-+upping+the+stakes

Using Class of Service to Manage Risk in Innovative New Product Development

by

Siddharta Govindaraj, siddharta@silverstripesoftware.com

and

Sreekanth Tadipatri, sreekantht@agilefaqs.com

ABSTRACT

Traditional Agile processes don't have a systematic framework for managing product risk. Risk management is instead delegated to Product Owners and ScrumMasters to be managed implicitly. Unfortunately, when risk is not make visible it is handled in an ad hoc manner.

Kanban makes risk explicit and visible using "class of service" categories. Classes of service are combined with explicit policies to handle different work items differently. This allows businesses to manage risk in a project in a way that is not possible with traditional Agile methods.

Innovative new products operate in an environment of high uncertainty and are exposed to a number of product risks. Effective risk management is critical to ensuring product success. In this paper, we will discuss how we use classes of service to manage risk in innovative new product development.

INTRODUCTION

One of the most important aspects of innovation is design and launch of new products and services (Hauser et al, 2006). New product development is a relatively risky activity (Kahraman, Buyukozkan, & Ates, 2007; Kayis, Arndt, & Zhou, 2006; Ozer, 2001) as a result of market competition and product technology advancement.

The responsibility of managing these kinds of product risks falls on the shoulders of the Product Owner. In some projects, that could be a single person. In others, it could be a whole cross-functional product management team comprising of stakeholders, marketing staff, senior developers, and others. In this paper we are going to use the term Product Owner to mean any person, or group of people, who are responsible for building the right product and ensuring that the business gets the expected benefits of the project.

Product Owners are a single point of failure in agile processes. All the benefits of agile software development and agile project management rest on one critical assumption — that the Product Owner does a good job aligning development teams with business needs. If that doesn't happen, then it doesn't matter if you have the best agile team doing continuous deployments and one week sprints — you're just doing to deliver the wrong product faster to market.

In order to manage product risk, we need to first understand sources of risk. In this paper, we consider three sources of risk. These are:

- Risks due to uncertainty
- Risks due to poor business-development alignment, leading to the development team spending too much time on unimportant features, or too little time on critical features
- Risks due to delays

One mistake in new product development is to create a backlog of features and then treat every feature in exactly the same way. Different features are exposed to different kinds of risk. Each risk requires a different mitigation strategy. This means that different features need different workflow depending upon the risk it is exposed to. In this paper, we describe how class of service framework along with associated policies helps us do that.

RISK DUE TO UNCERTAINTY

Features in new product development are exposed to two types of uncertainty: market uncertainty and technology uncertainty. Market uncertainty is when you deliver a feature, but you aren't sure whether the feature will be accepted or wanted by your customers. Technology uncertainty is when there is a doubt on whether you will be able to build the feature in the first place. In addition to these, there are many well understood features that have neither of these uncertainties. We call these commodity features.

The backlog typically consists of a combination of uncertainty (market or technology) and commodity features. In such cases, the risk mitigation is to reduce uncertainty. The uncertainty arises from a lack of knowledge, either of the market or the technology. Therefore, it is important to focus on learning rather than delivery.

For market risk, you'll want to build out cheap prototypes of core features and get potential users to use it and give their feedback. For technology risk, you'll want to focus on spikes that explore the solution space in a quest to understand how the product can be built.

In both cases, iterations are important; you want to get the cycle time really short so that you can iterate to the right solution. The early backlog will have a lot of spikes. Quality is secondary. There is no point taking extra time to build a better quality prototype using test driven development or write a whole lot of automated functional tests, because there is a high probability that you will need to throw away many parts of the solution and start over again. Similarly, don't get stuck on the fact that you haven't delivered end user business value for a few weeks, because that isn't the point here.

RISK DUE TO BUSINESS NON-ALIGNMENT

From a business point of view, features are not all equal. Some features are very important to the success of the project, whereas others are unimportant. This is different from business value. You can have unimportant features which have a high business value, for example. An example is a login feature in a web application. The feature has high business value; your application cannot be released without it. Yet, it is unimportant for the success of your product. As long as it works, customers will not base purchase decisions on the quality of the login implementation.

A useful model for analyzing your product backlog in this way is the Kano model. The Kano model can be used to categorise features into three buckets: Basic (also called Hygiene), Performance (also called Linear), and Excitement (also called Differentiator). The image below shows how customer satisfaction varies with the quality of implementation for these three categories of features.

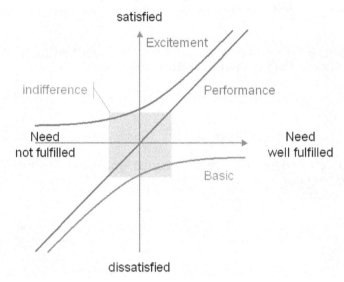

Kano Model from Wikipedia

Basic features: Basic features are features that lead to dissatisfaction if the feature is not present, but do not add to customer excitement when available. The login example described earlier is a basic feature.

Linear features: Linear features are features that fall into the "more is better" category. If you have more linear features, the customer feels proportionately better. For example, the number of camera file formats that are supported by a photo editing application are linear. If one app supports 10 camera models and another supports 20 models, it adds to the customer satisfaction linearly.

Differentiating features: These features are high excitement features that set you apart from the competition. A few differentiating features can offset the absence of many linear features, because they generate excitement for the customer. Marketing campaigns and product positioning for the product may be based on these features.

It helps to know the composition of the backlog based on these three categories. If you know that, then you can apply different strategies to each type of feature. For example, basic features are not worth spending too much time on. Implement them, make sure they work, and then move on. Differentiating features, on the other hand, are worth spending a lot more time on to get them right. You may want to call in some expert users to try them out during development, or run them through a couple of iterations of user experience trials before development starts. Linear features might fall somewhere in between.

If you put every feature on the backlog through the exact same development process, then you are likely doing your stakeholders a disservice. You are either wasting too much time on basic features, or spending too little time on differentiating features (or both).

The cost of delay model

Cost of delay is a model to examine the cost to the business if a particular feature is delayed. This can help product owners understand the time sensitivity of a feature and aid in prioritizing it appropriately.

Normal: Normal features have a linear cost of delay. If you deliver earlier, you can start getting the business benefits earlier. If you deliver later, then it costs the business more or less proportional to the time it was postponed.

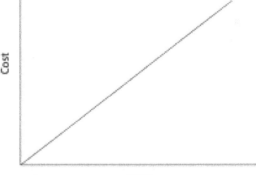

Expedite: Expedited features have a constant, high cost of delay. They are typically emergencies that have to be implemented immediately. Emergency production bug fixes might fall into this category.

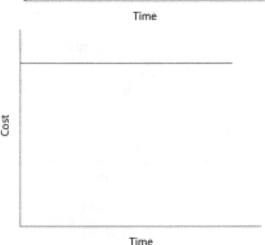

Fixed Date: Some features have a fixed date by which the feature has to be ready. It could be to meet a regulatory deadline or to launch a feature at a conference. These types of features have no cost of delay up to the deadline. There is no benefit to be gained by completing the feature early. If the deadline is missed though, it becomes costly.

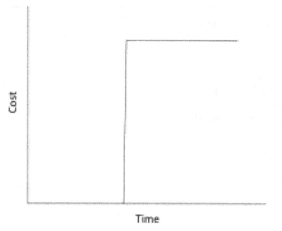

Intangible: Intangible features are long term features that have no immediate need to be implemented, but are required for the long term competitiveness of the project. For instance, up-grading the build and changing the architecture are features that fall into this category.

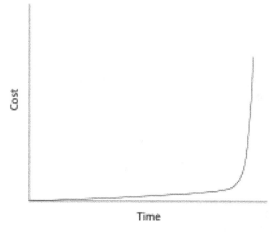

Once you know which bucket a feature falls into, then it makes prioritization decisions much easier. Obviously expedite features have to go to the top of the backlog. Fixed date features can be scheduled later, but with a buffer to ensure that they don't miss the deadline. Normal features fill in the other parts of the backlog, and intangibles are scheduled such that they are worked on during periods of downtime.

Using Cost of Delay to manage product risk

As we have seen so far, it makes sense to change the way we develop a feature based on the type of risk to which it is exposed. Kanban uses something called a Class of Service to abstract this idea.

At a simple level, class of service is just a bucket or category that you can use to catego-rize the features. For example, these seven classes encapsulate the three sources of risk de-scribed so far:

Class of service	Criteria
Expedite	Emergency bug fixes that need to be fixed and deployed in a few days.
Fixed Date	Features that have a fixed deadline.
High Uncertainty	Features exposed to market or technical risk. May take a few iterations to get right.
Basic	Basic features from the Kano model
High Value	Differentiating features from the Kano model.
Slack	Intangible, long term improvements to be picked up during times of slack.
Normal	Everything else.

One advantage of class of service is that it can be coupled with policies to handle different classes in different ways. Policies can be designed in such a way that they are aligned to business expectations.

For example, expedited items have a high cost of delay and need to be deployed as soon as possible. A policy for the expedite class could be something like this:

Expedite
- Only for emergency bug fixes
- Moves to the head of backlog and all queues
- Can override work in progress limits
- Team members stop whatever they are working on and swarm to complete this work item

This policy ensures that expedited items are deployed as fast as possible. Similarly, policies can be designed for the other classes to align them with the risk mitigation strategy.

Class of service can also be used to set schedule expectations. Measure the cycle time on work items for each class of service. You will then be able to visualize work items on a statistical process control chart and set expectations on the mean and upper bounds for items in that class. For example, you might find expedited items have a low mean and variation, whereas the high value class items may have a high mean and more variation. This is useful because it sets the expectation that there could be a lot of variation in certain classes, something that is not conveyed clearly when using single point estimates like days or story points.

Another advantage of class of service is that it allows you to quickly see the risk profile of the upcoming work items at a glance. If you have too many "High Uncertainty" work items, then that could be an indication that you might be taking on too much risk. Similarly, it is probably a good idea to mix Basic features with one or two High Value features that tie in with the business' market strategy.

This perspective leads to other strategies like breaking up large High Uncertainty features into smaller High Uncertainty features. You can then spread out the smaller features across multiple releases and "amortise" the risk over time.

CONCLUSION

Features in a product are not homogenous. Different features have different types of value and are exposed to different risks. This in turn requires teams to adopt different workflows depending on the type of feature. Managing these differences may be key to realising successful outcomes in highly competitive environments such as new product delivery.

Class of service coupled with explicit policies helps Product Owners develop a gut feel of the amount of risk associated with the backlog and take appropriate action. It also helps the development team to understand the context of a feature and self-organise in a way that aligns with business needs for that feature.

REFERENCES

Hauser, J., Tellis, G. J. and Griffin, A. (2006). "Research on Innovation: A Review and Agenda for Marketing Science", Marketing Science, vol. 25, no. 6, pp. 687.

Kahraman, C., Buyukozkan, G., & Ates, N. Y. (2007). A two phase multi-attribute decision-making approach for new product introduction. Information Sciences, 177(7), 1567-1582.

Kayis, B., Arndt, G., & Zhou, M. (2006). Risk quantification for new product design and development in a concurrent engineering environment. CIRP ANNALS Manufacturing Technology, 55(1), 147-150.

Ozer, M. (2001). Factors which influence decision making in new product evaluation. European Journal of Operational Research, 163 (3), 784-801.

Organic, not Chaotic: How to Grow your Architecture

by

Liz Keogh, liz@lunivore.com

ABSTRACT

Lean software development teams aim to reduce cycle time and get feedback fast. This sometimes brings teams into conflict with software architects, whose concern is more strategic. Traditionally, Enterprise Architects have drawn up large plans meant to survive many years. The implementation of such vast plans then slows down development teams, preventing them from realising the benefits of an iterative approach and its quick feedback. However, not all aspects of an architectural vision will be needed in the first or subsequent releases. By making a minimum commitment and paying to keep options open for later, a team can grow its architecture incrementally. Focusing on risk and phrasing the benefits of architecture in terms of business goals helps a team prioritise architectural components alongside regular work. This can also help a team to define tests, moving the role of an architect from one of gatekeeper to one of educator, and reducing rework accordingly.

ARCHITECTURE IN THE WILD

Software development projects are hard at the best of times. Our main stakeholders are users, and users are hard to please. Yet when we examine who the real stakeholders of a project are — starting with the primary stakeholders who created the project vision or provided the budget, and then considering all the other individuals, teams, departments, or bodies whose approval, support, or verification is needed to see the vision become reality — a different picture emerges. Projects frequently have many different stakeholders, often with competing requirements.

Ask the developers working on any large Enterprise projects which stakeholders give them the most stress and the least support, and one word often bubbles up to the top: *Architecture*.

In correlation, Enterprise Architects often find themselves isolated, frustrated, and desperate; they are responsible for strategic plans intended to align IT with current and future business needs, and forced to rely on the whims of development teams, with mixed abilities and tight deadlines, to deliver them.

Over the last decade this conflict has become exacerbated. Lean and Agile practices allow teams to adopt fast turn-around times, focusing on what they need to deliver incrementally. Developers quote Agile sayings and practices — "You ain't going to need it", "We have a flat cost of change", "Keep it simple, stupid" — and continue to chase fast feedback and throughput, often gaining the admiration and support of primary stakeholders and CIOs alike as they showcase their bold new way of working.

Meanwhile, architects throw up their hands in frustration. Years of experience teach them that once an application goes live, the chances of persuading the business stakeholders to give up yet more time and money for longer-term goals that may not even benefit their department directly are slim. They spend increasing amounts of time communicating their strategy and selling the benefits, only to spend the rest of their time watching as urgent deadlines and the cost of delay scupper their best laid plans.

It doesn't have to be this way.

THE PROBLEM

Enterprise Architecture is largely seen as a technology problem. When a company has created a separate architecture team, it often sits within the IT department as a separate function to both development and operations. It has no correlation within the business.

Conway's law states:

> "...organizations which design systems ... are constrained to produce designs which are copies of the communication structures of these organizations."

Without a corresponding function within the business, architects cannot obtain the support they need for their strategies. Combined with competition for budgets, lack of collaboration between departments, and a focus on cutting costs or increasing ROI, it becomes difficult, if not impossible, for architects to make any headway. Architecture provides options for flexibility in the future; it does not tend to produce profit. A company may not see benefit from its architectural investment for some years, if at all.

The second aspect to this problem is that architectural forces in software act continually in opposition to the first problem. High-level business stakeholders would like to see architecture provide solutions to the lack of communication, often by creating software that automates the processes requiring it, rendering human-to-human communication unnecessary. Yet when existing manual processes are modelled for the purposes of automation, these dysfunctions are captured, rather than eliminated.

The third problem is that architecture is seen as a problem, to which a solution must be found.

The last problem is that architects, like any other human beings, sometimes get it wrong — and they're right to worry about the cost of changing it later.

GETTING IT RIGHT UP FRONT

In 1970, Dr. Winston W. Royce outlined a method of working in which each stage provided more detailed requirements, followed by code, and then testing. He went on to say, "...the implementation... is risky and invites failure." [1] We now know this process as the "Waterfall" model of software delivery and — at least amongst most of those reading this — we know it as flawed.

Yet the same philosophy and process for which we actively seek alternatives remains one of the most prevalent ways of planning and producing architecture, even in companies making the transition from Waterfall to more iterative delivery cycles. If we were able to predict with any certainty what a particular business would be doing in five years, what performance it would require, and how its applications and collaborating systems would communicate with one another, then investing up-front in architecture would be a sound choice. Unfortunately, we aren't very good at prediction. For that reason, architects spend a lot of time evaluating technologies, trying to understand the strategic direction of a company and making the best prediction that they can, so that they have to change as little as possible.

Yet few architectural teams seem willing to admit the reality — that they cannot see the future, and that architecture will need to change accordingly. The investment made in the architectural vision, as with requirements in Waterfall, makes changes later on far more expensive than they would otherwise have been. The big investment up-front is actually *causing* the high cost of change that the investment seeks to avoid.

Many papers have already been written on alternatives; on incremental solutions which allow an architecture to evolve. The concept of incremental architecture has been around for decades. So why are so few companies doing it?

ASSUMING WE GOT IT WRONG

If we make the assumption, up-front, that our architecture strategy is flawed from the start, we practice it in a different way. These principles are the same as those used in incremental software development:

- Keep our options open.
- Get feedback quickly.

Another set of related principles can be found in Real Options, as espoused by Chris Matts and Olav Maasen[2]:

- Options have value.
- Options expire.
- Never commit early unless you know why.

With this in mind, we can also *pay* to keep our options open until we've had feedback and have more information with which to commit. This principle is commonly in practice wherever effort is put into flexible design, but is rarely explicitly called out. A particular practice that Chris Matts, a well-known Real Options practitioner, taught me was: "Don't pick the right technology. Pick the technology which is cheapest to move away from." In this way, we can make it OK to be wrong.

There are two more principles related to being wrong that have been the focus of fewer teams, especially within architecture, and that are also relevant:

- Do the risky stuff first.
- Write a test before you write the code.

These last two, applied to architecture, change the game.

Do the risky stuff first

The Kanban community uses the concept of a Business Value Increment or Minimum Marketable Feature, meaning the smallest thing that we can deliver.

Most people working in an incremental fashion still do so with backlogs of stories which are then prioritised, with the highest value items going forward. This is the practice particularly of Scrum or XP teams, in which either the scope or the deadline can be negotiable. It allows teams to ship partly-completed visions, with the most valuable capabilities and features first.

Prioritizing for deadline

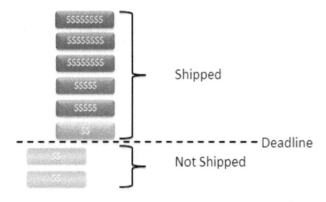

Figure 1 - Prioritising for a deadline, with most valuable features first

Once the vision is narrowed down to its absolute minimum, prioritising in this way no longer makes sense. If we could ship fewer high-value features, then that would define the vision instead. Some teams are now focusing on ignorance and risk, instead of value, and this allows them to start addressing *all* the risk, for all stakeholders, including architecture.

MMF or BVI – less time to $

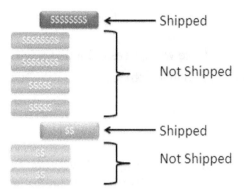

Figure 2 - Using MMF or BVI, where the most risky features are often the most differentiating and potentially most valuable

Things that aren't risky can then be added later, once feedback on the most risky aspects has been received. We focus first on the areas in which we are ignorant, and then on the areas that are risky — recognising that a known appreciation of risk merely means that there are *some* bits about which we're ignorant, or at least, can't predict.

Risky aspects of architecture include:

- Anything about which the project team is ignorant.
- Anything that might not work at all.
- Anything that has been known to be risky elsewhere.
- Anything involving complex interactions with other components.

Risky aspects of architecture rarely include things with which the team are familiar, and that they've done before. This also gives the team a focus on learning, with the maximum time available to adapt to any surprises.

The shortcuts that teams have taken in order to get feedback on more risky aspects of architecture may be surprising — and alarming — to architects. However, since a minimum vision may turn out to be wrong or not viable, taking shortcuts like these can represent the greatest learning for the least investment:

- Hard-coded users - no logins, because login mechanisms are well understood.
- Hard-coded server-side data - because getting data out of a database is easy.
- Hard-coded client-side data - because we already have some server-side data to prove the architecture with.
- Deployments to one server instead of many - because we can easily deploy to many servers later.
- Deployments in one package instead of many - because we can easily split packages later.
- Fake domain objects - because the understanding of domain objects is less risky than the architecture required to support them.
- Map-based caching strategies - because more complex strategies can be evaluated later.
- Etc.

These shortcuts come from anecdotal as well as personal experience, and have resulted in successful adoptions of new architecture, incrementally, from the most risky aspects through to a viable MMF. The actual shortcuts taken by teams have depended on team members' technical knowledge and their context, with the team conversing with architectural and business stakeholders to identify "the things that stop you sleeping at night".

Write a test before you write the code

Real Options suggests that we should seek information before we make a commitment. In Behavior Driven Development (BDD) we use natural language and conversational patterns around how users might use an application to encourage discovery of scenarios before the commitment of implementation is made. Testers in a team practicing BDD will find themselves engaged before the code is written to help developers and analysts uncover misunderstandings and gaps in analysis, where traditionally their only input came in the form of rework.

Traditional

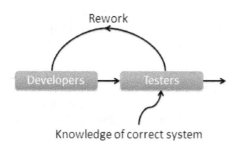

Figure 3 - Traditional processes in which testing happens after the commitment of implementation

BDD

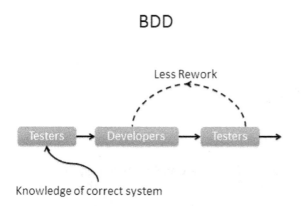

Figure 4 - BDD process in which scenarios are discussed before implementation

Traditionally, Architects have taken a gatekeeping role. They communicate the architecture to the developers, and then tell the developers if they've done it wrong. In a similar way to the turn-around made by testers in BDD, we can use conversations around architectural scenarios and tests to avoid the rework often suffered by developers in long evenings and weekends close to the deadline. We can also hijack user scenarios as a "walking skeleton" to explore which bits of an architecture are truly needed for the quick feedback that the rest of the business craves.

A familiar example of a kind of architectural test might be one of performance. However, performance tests are often used speculatively, with software being reworked when the performance is "not good enough". By defining required performance metrics ahead of the implementation, the development team members can put automated tests in place to tell them when something they do breaks the necessary performance — and to allow them to fix the problem cheaply, close to where it was created.

Often the business stakeholders are unsure of why they are paying for architectural features, often seen as "technical". By phrasing each feature in terms of the stakeholder who benefits, it becomes easier to sell the architecture at the same time as defining the test. We can use the Feature Injection template, taken from a set of practices also proposed by Chris Matts, which deliberately discover misunderstandings in the higher levels of analysis.

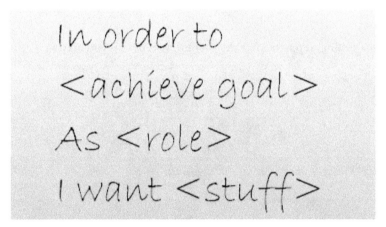

Figure 5 - the Feature Injection template

This is similar to the User Story template created by Mike Cohn[iii]: "As a user, I want <stuff>, so that <goal>" - but in contrast to the "so-that", often used optionally, the goal is explicitly defined and comes first. We also do not necessarily consider the user to be the only stakeholder involved. Many user-oriented requirements are actually provided for the benefit of other stakeholders - online advertisements, for instance.Consider these examples, which play directly into the architecture of the system:

- In order to retain customers, as the Head of Customer Service, I want staff to be able to find customer details in less than 10 seconds.

- In order to prevent stale data from being used, as the Head of Trading, I want the app to disable itself within five seconds of the pricing server going down.

- In order to comply with government regulations, as the Head of Audit, I want to know who changed the data and when.

Not only have we explicitly defined tests — customer details in less than 10 seconds, five-second disabling, able to tell who changed what data — but we have also captured the business benefit that each aspect of the architecture provides. The actual mechanism by which the architecture achieves the goal is left as a collaborative decision between the architects and the development team. In some cases, architects play an active part in the team's implementation, sitting alongside them, pair-programming with them, and helping them to adopt the relevant aspects of the vision.

By placing these stories on a Kanban board, we can make them visible to all interested stakeholders and help them to understand why we are taking the time to implement these aspects of the architecture. This can help stakeholders collaborate, fixing some of the communication issues without even implementing architecture to do so. We can also provide the architects with either automated or manual tests, helping them engage better with the team and provide further education going forward.

CONCLUSION

There is no silver bullet for Enterprise Architecture. Change will always happen, and will always have an associated cost. However, by following some simple principles, the chances of successfully adopting a more flexible, incremental approach which allows for faster feedback are increased.

- **Accept that change will be required** and pay to keep options open by creating minimum commitments, deliberately discovering knowledge through conversation, and recognising flexible design as a mechanism for enabling future change.

- **Prioritise by ignorance and risk** in order to improve the rate at which a team learns, get feedback quickly, and leave the maximum time left to adapt to any surprises.

- **Focus on the business value of architecture** in order to engage stakeholders more effectively and help them to collaborate.

- **Move architects from a gatekeeping role to an educational one**, creating tests that the team can use to determine if their architectural solutions match the stated goals.

While incremental architecture itself might be a technology problem, the barriers to adopting it exist within people and their organisations. It can benefit us to act accordingly.

REFERENCES

i Melvin Conway. How do Committees Invent?(1968) Retrieved from http://www.melconway.com/research/committees.html

ii Dr. Winston W. Royce. Managing the Development of Large Software Systems (1970). Retrieved from http://www.cs.umd.edu/class/spring2003/cmsc838p/Process/waterfall.pdf

iii Chris Matts and Olav Maasen. "Real Options" underlie Agile Practices (2007). *InfoQ*. Retrieved from http://www.infoq.com/articles/real-options-enhance-agility

iv Mike Cohn, Advantages of the "As a user, I want" User Story Template (2008). *author's blog*. Retrieved from http://blog.mountaingoatsoftware.com/advantages-of-the-as-a-user-i-want-user-story-template

Nothing to Hide, Nowhere to Run:

Making Your Organization Progress and Agile Transition Visible -

The Get it Done Guide

by

Jason Little

http://www.agilecoach.ca

ABSTRACT

"WTF?!? We've been agile for 3 months and I have no idea what's going on!"

That's the cleaned up quote from the CTO of a company I worked with in the past. Agile transitions create visibility around the work that is being done, and typically this visibility is limited to team task boards and other team-level information such as burn-down charts. Organizations generally rely on three levels of planning: strategic, tactical, and operational. While having team-level (operational) data made visible is a good start, it's not enough to give managers and executives the data they need to make strategy, product, and project decisions.

Typically organizations use status updates, documents, tools, and meetings to flow information up and down the hierarchy. From my experience, the flow of data goes through many filters while traversing the hierarchy and it's not uncommon for a more positive picture to be painted of projects the further up the hierarchy the data goes.

The objective of making data more visible is to generate "why" questions that help challenge the status quo, which will lead to smarter business decisions. This "Get it Done" guide will give you ideas of how to determine what data is relevant for each of the three levels of planning and also make you aware of organizational impacts that come along with making previously hidden data visible in your organization.

GET IT DONE - QUICK START GUIDE

This guide is designed to give you enough information to get started. These are the steps I've found helpful mixed in with a couple of stories so you can hopefully avoid some of the mistakes I've made while creating visibility. Let's quickly define "visible." By this I mean **big visible charts** posted on the walls in your office, not visible in a wiki that nobody sees. While sticky notes may appear non-professional and childish, they are cheap, quick, and efficient and most importantly they get bums out of the seats and walking around, which leads to better collaboration.

Step 1 - Create Awareness

I was working in an enterprise-sized company with a pilot Scrum team and we found that generally we'd lose 2-3 days per sprint waiting for infrastructure to be available. *"Oh, that's always the way it's been,"* said Joe, their lead programmer. *"We don't have integration environments and our development environments are owned by other departments so we're just stuck sometimes."* I made this data visible without considering the impact through our impediment log. The impact was two managers and a senior manager, ahem, not-so-politely conveying their unhappiness about making this information available to their superiors. In this example, the organization had a highly political culture. Process controlled the flow of this information, and the system was designed in a way to be able to hide this information due to the repercussions it could cause.

Before making data more visible in the organization, create awareness about what data will be made visible, and why, and create personal safety for those who will likely be affected by it.

Step 2 - Decide what data is relevant

Does a CTO care about a team-level burn-down chart? Probably not. Decide what data your organization needs to see from a strategic, tactical, and operational perspective. The angry CTO from the abstract had no idea what was being released, and with 11 teams running in Scrum or Kanban processes, traveling to each team board to compile data wasn't something he had time for, and neither did the managers. The first step was to create a matrixed release wall, which you'll see later on in this article, to provide a snapshot of what was being done in the engineering and operations departments.

Step 3 - Get Buy-In

Whether you are a manager, external coach/consultant, or internal process coach, make sure you have buy-in from the people who are responsible for generating this data. The teams need to own making their progress visible to management and management needs to own making impediment removal and organizational goals visible. If the people in the organization do not own making their parts visible, you may as well post status reports to that old wiki that nobody uses. As a change agent, I've found it helpful to observe the organization and create some examples of visible data as a training tool. Ask questions like *"If you had this data, would you be able to make smarter hiring decisions?"*

Step 4 - Decide what to do with the data

While working for a medium-sized company, our coaching team had problems getting one particular group kicked off using Scrum. We were delayed with training efforts and there just didn't seem to be a right time to get started. Once we got started with Scrum, we found we kept getting interrupted by production issues. After a few sprints we accepted reality and switched to Kanban, as the work was too unpredictable to plan in two-week sprints. We discovered that for every one issue we solved, two would replace it, and about 99% of the team's time was spent on production support or maintenance. This data helped us decide to only focus on critical issues and to ignore the already large backlog so we could implement a root-cause process to figure out why we had so many production issues. After three months we reduced the time spent on support and maintenance to 95%. Big deal some will say, however, progress is progress and we needed to start somewhere.

By using similar visibility techniques in other groups, we created quarterly A3 reports within the engineering group to support non-product work that would contribute towards fixing the infrastructure and underlying code problems.

BIG VISIBLE CHARTS - AGILE TRANSITION WALL

Start off with making your Agile transition visible. Whether you have external coaches/ consultants or an internal Agile rollout team, having this team make its work visible is a great way to model the behavior of making work visible. In a larger organization it helps to provide information to many people in the organization as efficiently as possible, as the coach or consultant may not be able to spend a great deal of time with multiple teams.

Agile Transition Team Board: Helps model the behavior of making work visible, helps to communicate with the rest of the organization what is happening with the Agile transition.

Upcoming Events: Helps generate interest in Agile, socializes events designed to help create a self-sustaining culture.

Team Status: Helps shows multi-team progress, in the example below, seeing *"Team 3 - Too Busy to Start"* will lead to questions like:

Why are they too busy to start? - They're too busy to start because they have a high support load.

Why do they have a high support load? - Because the releases are too frequent and testing isn't finished in time, which leads to insufficiently tested features and more inbound support calls.

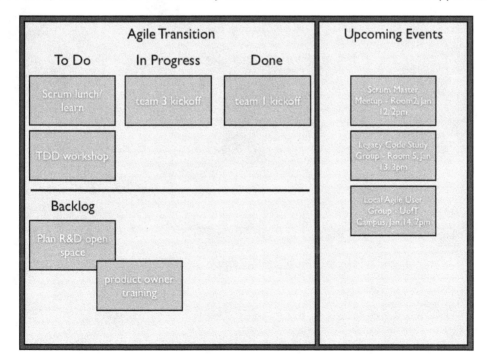

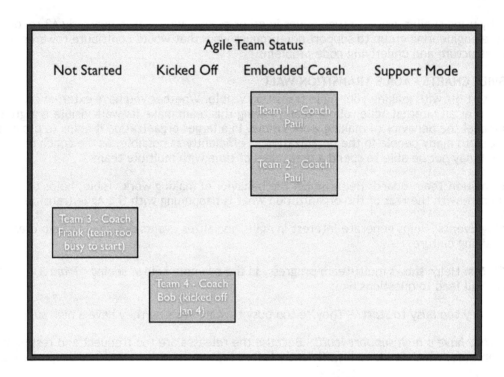

TEAM TASK BOARDS AND INFORMATION WALLS

Team level information such as task boards, burn-down charts, and impediment logs are a great way to help managers see what's happening at the team level. It's also helpful in a multi-team environment to do "Agile Safari" so teams can visit other teams and see how they are managing their work.

Task board: Team task boards help make visible the work that the team is doing. The team may be working on multiple projects; they may also be handling maintenance and support. Knowing what the team is working on helps with organizational alignment and also allows the team to manage its own work. In the example below, the team is handling production support and two versions of the product. CMS V3.0 may be the most important release; however, emergency work is being done in the old version. This data can help management see the team's reality. While V3.0 may be the most important, the day-to-day reality is that there is a high demand on V2.5 features that all clients are running.

Team Information Wall: Teams will develop working agreements and generate improvements from their retrospectives as well as impediments. Having this information is helpful to remind the team about its agreements and follow-up actions from the retrospective. From the team's perspective, making impediments visible helps keep the manager or Scrum Master accountable for removing those obstacles.

Agile Safari: In a multi-team environment, some teams may be using Scrum, others Kanban, and from my experience, teams form working agreements and make tweaks to their processes. In a multi-team environment it can be helpful for teams to see how other teams are working. "Agile Safari" is simply a term for getting people to walk around and see how other teams are operating.

I was working with a team handling product development and support and they were really struggling with their process. Let's call them the Alpha team. Scrum wasn't working well for them, and they heard one of the maintenance teams was having success with a "Scrumban" type of process. A few people from the struggling team went to go see how they were working to get some ideas. That sparked the "Agile Safari" term and other teams started wandering around seeing how other teams were working.

Visiting other teams was a great experience for the Alpha team. Soon afterwards they had redefined their process, created a simpler Kanban board and process, and other teams started coming to them to see how they had improved.

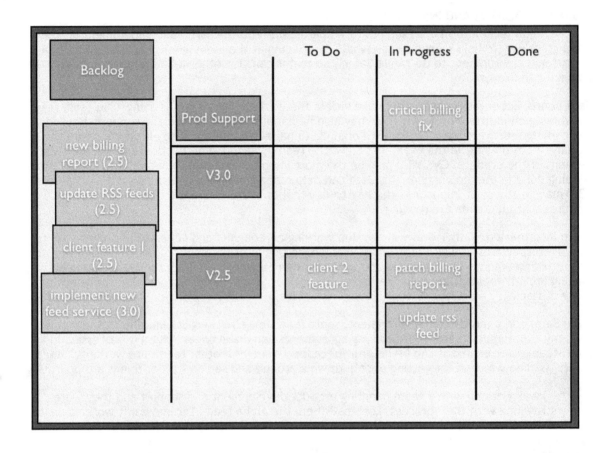

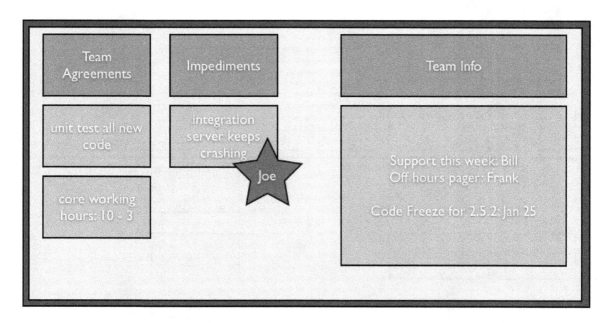

ROLLED UP TEAM DATA, RELEASE, AND OPERATIONAL INFORMATION

The release and operational information wall can be considered the "one stop shop" for managers to know what's going on with the product, development, support, and maintenance.

Rolled up Team Data: This information can be as simple as showing a list of upcoming team demo sessions with bullet points of what will be shown at the demo. This is a great way for sales and marketing to see a snapshot of what is being done, as well as a way to keep the teams accountable for their commitments.

Release Information: In a multi-team environment, many teams may be working on the same product and have instances where changes made by Team 1 can break the changes made by Team 2. Having a release information wall and conducting a *"Scrum of Scrums"* stand-up in front of this wall can help teams stay coordinated and aware of what work is being done by other teams.

Operational Information - Support and Maintenance Requests: Seeing a snapshot of inbound support and maintenance requests in addition to seeing release information can be helpful to managers who need to see what's happening within their development and operations groups. For example, suppose this wall shows that support requests keep going up. This can lead to a root cause analysis of what areas of the product generate the most support requests. This can lead to a focus on reducing support calls by understanding what customers are calling about and then fixing the underlying product areas.

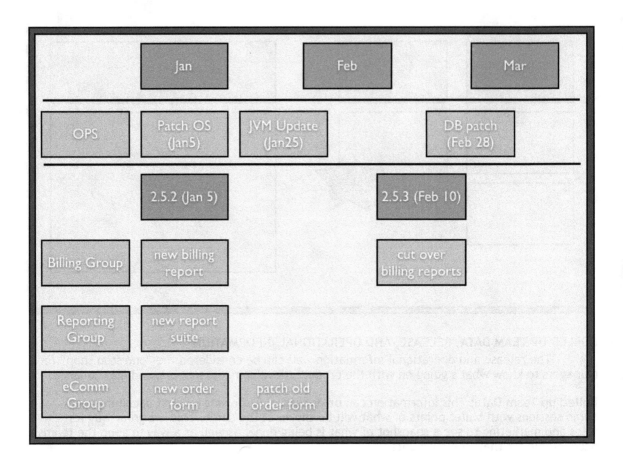

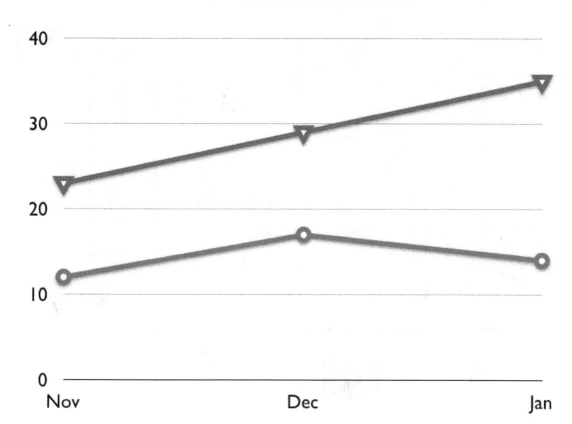

REAL WORLD EXAMPLES - THE BIG PICTURE

The image below shows the layout of the building and where the big visible charts were for a medium sized company I worked with.

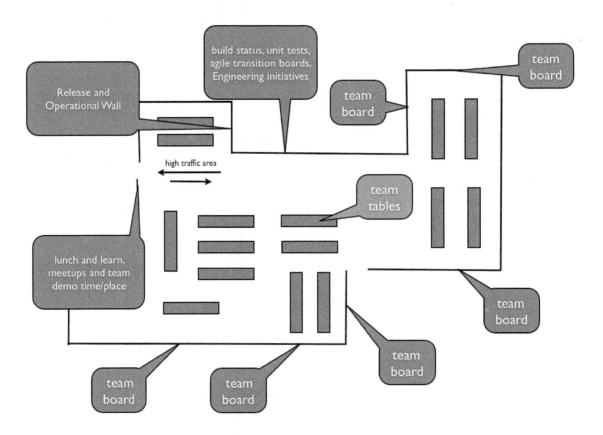

REAL WORLD EXAMPLES - HOW'S OUR COMPANY DOING?

Below is an example of a visible chart that shows closed sales versus live clients versus inbound support cases. This chart shows that closed sales is starting to excel at a rate greater than the professional service team can keep up with. It's also showing that support isn't an issue because more clients are going live, yet support is still flat.

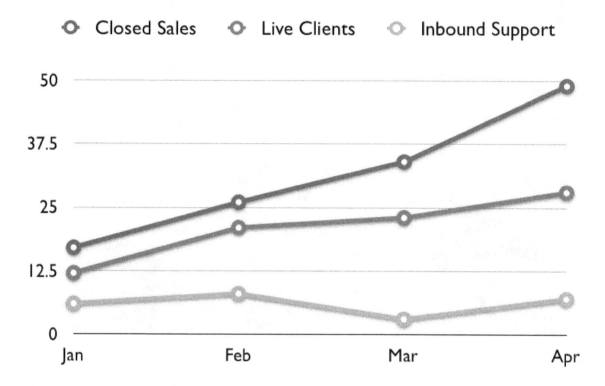

In this case, this information helped the organization realize it is going to exceed its ability to keep up with demand and need to increase capacity or find and cut out waste in the production system. Before making this visible it just *"felt like"* there was a lot of work to do.

REAL WORLD EXAMPLES - THE RELEASE WALL

CONCLUSION

Organizations rely on three levels of planning: strategic, tactical, and operational. Making your Agile transition and organizational progress visible will lead to breaking down functional silo walls and will allow for better decisions across these levels of planning. To be successful, first create awareness about the value of making data visible in your organization. Avoid mandating visibility; it simply will not work, and above all else, create personal safety for the people affected.

Making previously hidden data visible in your organization can be challenging and it will disrupt the status quo. Before getting started, ask yourself a simple question: Are you satisfied with how your business is working right now?

Value Innovation for Accelerated Competitive Advantage

and Organizational Maturity

by

Masa Kevin Maeda, masa@shojiki-solutions.com

ABSTRACT

Lean, agile, and Kanban are great approaches to improve organizations. Kanban, for example, facilitates the acceleration of enterprise maturity. The effectiveness of these approaches allows us to confront challenges when we consider how to improve factors such as leadership, customer interaction, communication and collaboration with other stakeholders, and so on. Furthermore, there is no specific consideration on how to obtain or increase competitive advantage (a key point to most businesses), nor on innovation, a growing factor in the business world. A Value Innovation framework that emphasizes the importance of innovation and how to put it into practice in the enterprise is proposed here. This framework takes as departure point the Lean-Agile Prism and has four components that contribute to increases in competitive advantage and organizational maturity. Value Innovation is sustainable, actionable, evolutionary, and increases intrinsic motivation, all of which contribute to increases in value flow.

INTRODUCTION

Every professional who has worked on more than one project eventually comes to the realization that no two projects are the same, and sooner or later comes to understand the real meaning of the phrase "there is no silver bullet". It doesn't take long to also realize that no two teams are the same. On the other hand we have standards, models, and methods developed to help us reduce the level of chaos in projects. Unfortunately, most of the time leaders and teams fall very quickly into *template* mode (take a standard, model, or method as a recipe where all you have to do is give values to the variables, and then everything will go as it should). Then they expect things to go right by simply *applying the rules,* apparently without realizing the contradiction between their realizations and their actions.

The combined use of lean thinking, agile thinking, and Kanban has proven to be a successful combination to better organizations. Both in my own practice and through reported accounts, I found that the success is not as broad and complete as is desirable by organizations because the scope is typically limited, e.g., within the confines of software development only. Other factors affecting the product development such as leadership, customer interaction, communication and collaboration with other stakeholders, increase of competitive advantage, and focus on innovation aren't given the level of attention necessary to increase success.

Throughout my extensive, international-level experience in the industry I have been gradually shaping up what I now call Value Innovation — the definition is provided later on this paper — as the result of my pursuit to figure out what the essential components are to keep individuals, teams, and organizations from falling into the *template* trap and to help them become as effective as possible in delivering value. Some of the key elements that allowed me to shape up value innovation were systems thinking, the system of profound knowledge, lean, agile, Kanban, and cognitive psychology.

First I will introduce the Lean-Agile Prism, which is an extension of the agile triangle that resulted from adding lean thinking. Next I will discuss value innovation by defining it and describing the framework and its parts. Last I will present one case where value innovation has been applied.

THE LEAN-AGILE PRISM

Motivation

I introduced a first version of the Lean-Agile Prism through an article for the "Agile Journal"[1] in April of 2010 and an improvement to it through an article for the "Cutter Consortium"[2] in June of 2010. I came up with it as result of applying lean thinking over the Agile Triangle[3] and have matured it to what I consider to be its final version presented here.

Let's say two new products have been launched to market. For the sake of the exercise let's assume they have been launched by two entirely new companies, with no history, no marketing or PR campaigns, and no other external influence factors, such that all we count with is the products themselves (see Figure 1). Both products offer the exact same value (functionality in this case) and the exact same level of quality. The question then is: Which one would you buy?

Figure 1: Two products of same value and quality

I have asked this question to close to 500 people in diverse contexts and the first answer most people give is "the cheapest one!" I then allow extra time and as people give different opinions the other prevailing decision criteria is "the one I like best!" If we explore the costs vs. looks criteria we will realize that far more people are willing to sacrifice cost over looks than the other way around. This means that cost is not as important to customers as it is considered for most projects. That is, if we pay more attention to increasing value to customer — such as in terms of design — we might end up doing better business.

The next step in the exercise is to consider another two products, again with no external factors. In this case the products offer the exact same level of value, quality, cost, and looks (see Figure 2). Of course, in a real-life case they would not look the same, but the point here is that they are equally attractive to customers. The question again is: Which one would you buy?

Figure 2: Two products of same value, quality, cost, and looks

Since there is no actual differentiator here, let's say that sales take place and after some time a market research shows that both companies sold the exact same number of units. Therefore, sales were equal. What then? Well, the company that had lower expenses wins because it ended up with larger profits.

The Lean-Agile Prism

In 2009 Jim Highsmith introduced the Agile Triangle[3], which tells us that Value, Quality, and Restrictions (cost, schedule, scope) are the right considerations to develop products. I agree with it and from the agile perspective I would say it is correct, but from the lean perspective I would say it is incomplete.

Let's consider the two exercises above. The first exercise is telling us that if an enterprise does innovation towards the customer then it is more likely to come up with a more attractive product, which might result in higher sales as result of the added value to customer. The second exercise is telling us that if an enterprise does innovation towards the way they design, develop, distribute, etc. the product then their costs might decrease, resulting in higher profit as result of the added value to the enterprise. The Agile Triangle talks about value to the customer. What I am proposing is to consider both value to customer and value to the enterprise, where value to the enterprise has to be in alignment to value to the customer. The result is the Lean-Agile Prism (Figure 3).

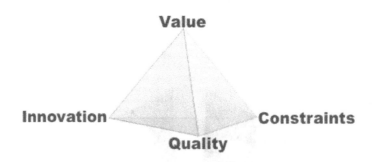

Figure 3: The Lean-Agile Prism

What the Lean-Agile Prism suggests is that by adding Innovation as another key factor in addition to those in the Agile Triangle we get a more complete reference framework to carry out successful projects, where value is towards both the customer and the enterprise, and value to enterprise is in alignment with value to customer. Value remains as the pinnacle of the structure because it is the most important factor of all. The other three are needed to maximize it.

VALUE INNOVATION

What is Value Innovation?

The term Value Innovation was coined by W. Chan Kim and Renée Mauborgne. Although I cannot reproduce their definition here due to copyright issues (first time I ran into a definition that had a copyright associated with it) what I can say is that it has to do with focusing on growing business by identifying new markets instead of focusing on competition. What I introduce here is slightly different but in alignment to a large degree with Kim and Mauborgne's definition. Therefore, using the same term is adequate.

Talking about innovation is risky because of the word itself. When do we innovate and when do we invent? When is something new and different an actual innovation? There is no definite answer. The way I would like us to think about innovation here is the act of taking as starting point elements we have available and coming up with something new that results in a positive change that adds value to customer or value to enterprise. That "something new" can be, say, a process, tool, or way to collaborate, and can be of any size and degree of simplicity.

Figure 4: Innovation: a significant positive change

In our context, value innovation is a framework for sustainable, actionable, and evolutionary activity that uses innovative thinking, innovation fostering environments, and innovative tools to accelerate competitive advantage and enterprise maturity. This means that with value innovation your organization can more easily achieve continuous value flow delivery and improves by building on top of its own successes.

It is worth mentioning that I am not attempting to systematize innovation, but rather proposing a set of elements that, when in place, would make it easier to innovate.

Innovative Thinking

The vast majority of the enterprises I have worked for or consulted to adopt lean-agile project management, Kanban, or scrum had a history of struggles with projects where strong communication and collaboration chaos prevailed. Leaders couldn't figure out what to do. Some of them had tried scrum to no avail — one of them also tried Kanban and the results were very discouraging to the team that applied — and were desperate. To me it was clear that the problem resided in something more profound that had nothing to do with their processes, corporate governance, or so on. The problem resided in the stakeholders themselves: the way they communicated and collaborated, but most importantly their state of mind. So I started adding two aspects to adoption strategies: Change their state of mind and put very strong emphasis on communication and collaboration. All that shaped up the innovative thinking part of value innovation and has had fabulous results, as I will show with the cases at the end of this paper.

Innovative thinking is a state of mind in which stakeholders:

- Are willing to accept and go through a transformation in the way they see and do their job. This is the first and most important step. There is no value innovation without it and each stakeholder in the organization that doesn't accept it becomes an element of friction that affects its positive impact.

- Apply Systems Thinking[4] to better understand what needs to be accomplished and to solve problems more effectively.

- Apply the System of Profound Knowledge[5] as a set of guidelines to improve management.

- Apply lean thinking to take advantage of its practicality to improve processes.

- Apply agile thinking to use innovative tools more effectively.

  Leaders apply psychology to better their teams internally and in their interaction with other groups and individuals. Those familiar with the system of profound knowledge might find this redundant. I emphasize on it however to make clear the tremendous importance it has to be able to generate permanent change.

The transformation of state of mind facilitates:

- The acknowledgement of the importance to count mavericks and challengers as part of the team. We want rebels with a cause, people who will question things and seek out new, better ways to do what needs to be done.

- The generation of intrinsic motivation as the main driving force to do good quality work. A high level of understanding, communication, and collaboration results in an increased sense of ownership and that sense of ownership increases intrinsic motivation.

- The understanding of the importance to focus on value to customer and value to enterprise.

Because innovative thinking fosters understanding, communication, and collaboration I would say that an organization that applies innovative thinking forms understanding workers instead of knowledge workers. The cultural change becomes easier and politics tend to become less important.

Furthermore, doing some work on Innovative Thinking before going about your adoption of Kanban or lean-agile management becomes easier.

Innovation-Fostering Environment

The second element to value innovation is to create an environment that fosters innovation. People doing lean or agile already have a good understanding of the importance of creating the right environment to succeed in applying their methodologies. The right environment brings the right human and material resources together in a way that allows people to innovate as easily as possible. An innovation-fostering environment:

- Makes it easy to communicate. Eliminate any aspects of your environment that create physical or psychological barriers of communication. Walls, protocols, titles, etc.

- Makes it easy for all stakeholders at all levels of the organization, including customers and end users, to collaborate. Have common areas for people to work together; adopt practices that require collaboration.

- Is transparent with respect to all aspects of the project and the organization. There is very little to actually hide from all stakeholders. The higher the level of knowledge all stakeholders have on every aspect of the project the more effective and motivated they'll be.

- Brings mavericks and challengers on board.

- Gives stakeholders slack to explore, try new things without fear of making mistakes, and dedicate time to adding value (to customer, enterprise, and themselves) and to increasing quality.

- Promotes autonomation[6]. The more you automate the more time people will have to make improvements over the product, processes, and the automation itself.

- Grants them autonomy. A pulling culture.

In an innovative environment leaders don't manage; they guide teams towards a common purpose whose result is the target product or service.

Innovative Tools

Tools are essential assets to get the job done, and in the case of value innovation it is highly advantageous to create tools that are not only innovative but that also assist in the innovation process. A great example of such a tool is the Kanban method[7]. It is innovative in a number of ways that increase team effectiveness and also promote improvements from stakeholders in contact with that team. At the same time, it provides visual tools and quantified evidence whose ease of generation and interpretation facilitate root cause analysis, giving more time to figure out how to make improvements. Even better, using innovative thinking and counting with an innovation-fostering environment makes it possible to go about doing Kanban more effectively. It makes it more natural to step back from the mechanics of the Kanban method and pay more attention to the understanding and the analysis of behaviors around it to come up with even better solutions and improvements.

Innovative tools are in alignment with autonomation and cover not only steps in the process but also the activities in between them. That is, it is encouraged to automate everything that makes sense to automate so that we focus human resources on activities that do require humans[8] to identify and boost improvements. Tools also increase autonomy and mastery, which in turn increase motivation.

Not all innovative tools are necessarily related to automation. Good examples of such tools are the planning poker[9] and innovation games[10].

The Value Innovation framework

We require innovative thinking, an innovation-fostering environment, and innovative tools to do value innovation. All three factors have a common denominator: the human factor. Innovative thinking is a transformation at human level; an innovation-fostering environment allows people to be more effective creating products or services while also innovating, and innovative tools boost people and systems performance.

But the human factor also has to do with pursuing an improvement of the human quality through our work activities, both towards the customer and towards the enterprise. The result of this is, quite coincidentally, that the Value Innovation framework is also a prism, with the human factor at the pinnacle.

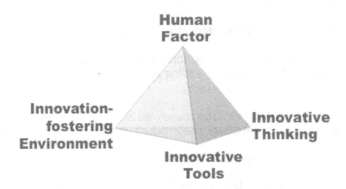

Figure 5: The Value Innovation Prism

The human factor also includes aspects such as stakeholder buy-in, counting with both and internal and an external champion for successful adoption such as agile methodologies, and leaders and champions as bridges to create human relation harmony between stakeholder groups and individuals. Value innovation results in what could be called disciplined chaos.

CASE

Software development services organization

Within the second half of 2010 a software development services company asked me to help them with their Kanban adoption. They had decided to use an ongoing eight-month project that was already in month four and struggling to be on track. Their contracting process took way too long and I ended up joining them towards the end of month seven. My suggestion was to take another project but the customer insisted we proceeded with that one. My initial assessment concluded the organization was highly dysfunctional. The company's issues included:

- Very poor communication and collaboration with customer. Meetings were actually arguments and finger-pointing rounds with very little value.

- Development team with poor communication and collaboration skills. Team members worked mostly in isolation despite being in an open, common area.

- Very poor testing. Based entirely in template-driven positive functional testing that covered 20% functionality at best.

- Very high degree of technical debt from legacy code. It had taken three full-time people one year and the code was still extremely brittle.

- Poor technical infrastructure. Insufficient servers, no test automation, and no continuous integration.

- Immature leadership that didn't communicate/collaborate. Command and control strategy.

As result the team was overworked, stressed, and with no motivation. There was a high degree of employee rotation also. Additionally, they had yet to receive specifications for most of the UI, and the customer said it would take three weeks to get them ready and available, giving the development team only one week to implement and deliver it because of a hard deadline with lots of money at stake.

I talked to the CEO and the customer to make them accept that there was no way they would finish on time. Their attitude was to deliver on time no matter what (which meant poor quality). Although my contract with them was for Kanban adoption I offered to help them make the best of the time left to improve the product while also going through the adoption. They accepted.

My first activity was to give the entire company (80 people) a presentation on lean-agile and systems thinking, during which I focused primarily on aspects that have to do with human factor, communication, and collaboration. This was with the objective to facilitate communication with stakeholders outside the team. I then took the team and did a series of exercises and games to get them to start communicating and also to bring a common understanding on the state of team and the project. By the end of the day they were already communicating better. I spent the next few days combining sessions on lean-agile and Kanban, and coaching the two managers in the team to help them learn to work well together and start leading the team more effectively.

Another interesting challenge was the customer, or so the managers and the CEO told me. I was told the customer lead was very difficult to deal with and was advised not to talk to him because he was unwilling to collaborate and was also against me being there to bring Kanban. Noticing he was a hyperactive person, I decided to get his attention by first having very short, casual encounters, and making sure to give him something of value at each one, including an invitation to a brown bag presentation I gave on value innovation. I also gave him an invitation to help him produce the requirements in far less time and with better quality. He attended my presentation, and working with his team we finished 40% of the requirements, doing paper prototyping, in one day and then they took it from there to finish what was originally to take three weeks. As a result, the customer lead and I had a private conversation where I explained to him more about the importance of being better involved and of good collaboration (which had to happen also from the development team side). Two days later, the customer lead took the initiative to give a presentation to the development team to describe the product in-depth.

I kept coaching the team on Kanban while also teaching them test strategies, helping them organize their test efforts by leveraging the entire team, getting into motion the establishment of continuous integration, coaching the managers, and bringing the customer team and the development team closer together. There was good progress in all fronts. Team members began working more closely together, titles were eliminated so that the organization was flat (except for one manager), and team members covered more than one function. Work was controlled and flow was established using Kanban. Requirement analysis and initial estimations to determine scope were done in collaboration with all stakeholders involved.

From the time adoption started the first intermediate release was late by one day; the second intermediate release was four days ahead of schedule. The final product was late by two weeks in part because the customer saw the opportunity to make improvements that would enhance user experience, and did this in agreement with the end user. The system had better quality than anticipated (the project had actually been considered to be entirely cancelled and they were prepared to accept losses when I reported the actual state of it when I did the original assessment). The user experience was so good that in two and a half months they had the system installed in three offices at different geographical locations.

The team is currently working on a new project and doing so in a better way. Since the end of my coaching they have been working regular hours and in good health, create with continuous integration and test automation is ongoing, quality has increased beyond their expectations (now in one month they get less defects than they used to get in one day), team member dependency has been virtually eliminated so time off is now doable. Kanban is helping them greatly, although they have yet to take full advantage of quantification. The relationship with the customer is better than ever, and the customer itself decided to adopt value innovation and Kanban.

CONCLUSION

The original concept of value innovation, as defined by Kim and Mauborgne, suggests that instead of competing we should search for new markets. This seems to be in contradiction with my concept of value innovation when I indicate that it accelerates competitive advantage. However, this is actually non-conflicting because the competitive advantage acceleration doesn't have to be in the same line of business. Innovation can be a big contributor on the identification of an important differentiator that opens a new market or increases an existing one.

Value innovation increases successful adoption of lean and agile methodologies by paving the road at the human factor level. Innovative thinking is the first step, as it facilitates transformation to happen. Innovation-fostering environments facilitate the adoption process from the collaboration and mechanical standpoints. Innovative tools increase the speed of innovation by reducing time consuming work and providing high value information.

Value innovation has a significant positive impact on an enterprise's cultural maturity. Also, the higher the increase of skills on systems thinking and psychology, the more effective a leader can be in the use of value innovation.

Value innovation can be applied in any context, technical or other, and at all levels of the organization.

REFERENCES

1. Maeda, Masa K. (2010). The Lean-Agile Prism: Going beyond the Agile Triangle. *Agile Journal*. April 2011. Retrieved March 1 from http://www.agilejournal.com/component/content/2803?task=view

2. Maeda, Masa K. (2010). The Agile Triangle evolves as a Lean-Agile Prism. *Cutter Consortium*. June 2011. Retrieved March 1 from http://www.cutter.com/content/project/fulltext/updates/2010/apmu1012.html

3. Highsmith, Jim. (2009). *Agile Project Management: Creating Innovative Products (2nd Ed.)*. Boston, MA: Addison Wesley.

4. http://en.wikipedia.org/wiki/Systems_thinking

5. http://en.wikipedia.org/wiki/W._Edwards_Deming

6. http://en.wikipedia.org/wiki/Autonomation

7. Anderson, David J. (2010). *Kanban: Successful evolutionary change for your technology business*. Blue Hole Press.

8. Wiener, Norbert (1988). *The human use of human beings: cybernetics and society*. Jackson, TN: Da Capo Press.

9. http://www.mountaingoatsoftware.com/topics/planning-poker

10. Hohmann, Luke (2006). *Innovation Games: creating breakthrough products through collaborative play*. Boston, MA: Addison Wesley.

Managing and Visualizing Non-linear Workflows Using a Kanban Matrix

by

Gerard Meszaros, LSSC2011@gerardmeszaros.com

ABSTRACT

Many approaches to building a Kanban board involve mapping the workflow and creating (at least) one column for each role or specialization. Each piece of functionality progresses in a sequential manner across the columns. This report describes the use of a different style of Kanban board, the Kanban Matrix, that can be used when the work can be done in many different orders or the tasks are too variable in size to achieve efficient one piece flow. Each cell in the matrix represents a potential task (a work type involved in delivering one item), and the status of the task is communicated using color and text. This allows tasks to be done in any order or even in parallel.

INTRODUCTION

I was working on the second draft of the book *xUnit Test Patterns* (Meszaros, 2007). The content was largely nailed down in the form of 19 smells and 69 patterns, a couple dozen sidebars, a dozen introductory chapters, plus a number of appendices spread across roughly 400 files. But there was an ever expanding list of edits (kinds of "things to do") to each chapter that I needed to keep track of. I initially broke the work out by chapter and defined "Finished" as having finished the complete list of edits on that chapter. But as I worked on subsequent chapters, I often found yet another edit to do to each chapter, including all the chapters that I had already "Finished". Also, many of the edits were fairly small and were more efficient to do on a group of chapters than to do to each single chapter separately, but they were still too large to do to *all* chapters at once. Furthermore, some edits could be done at the same time as others while other edits needed a different mindset. So I concluded that neither the chapter nor the edit was the optimal unit of work for single piece flow. As the number of edits climbed well past 10, and with over 400 files, the prospect of managing this work at the edit-per-file level was daunting.

INITIAL SOLUTION

I started out by building a classic XP-style (eXtreme Programming) planning board on the wall using Post-it™ whiteboard sheets. (See Cohn, Mike [2011] for more information.) I put up a sticky note for each chapter and created task stickies for the four or five edits that I had identified. (See *Figure 1-Classic XP-style task board.*) I started working on one chapter, applying each edit, and moving it across the columns as each edit was finished. When I finished the last edit, I moved the chapter sticky into the "Chapter Done" column.

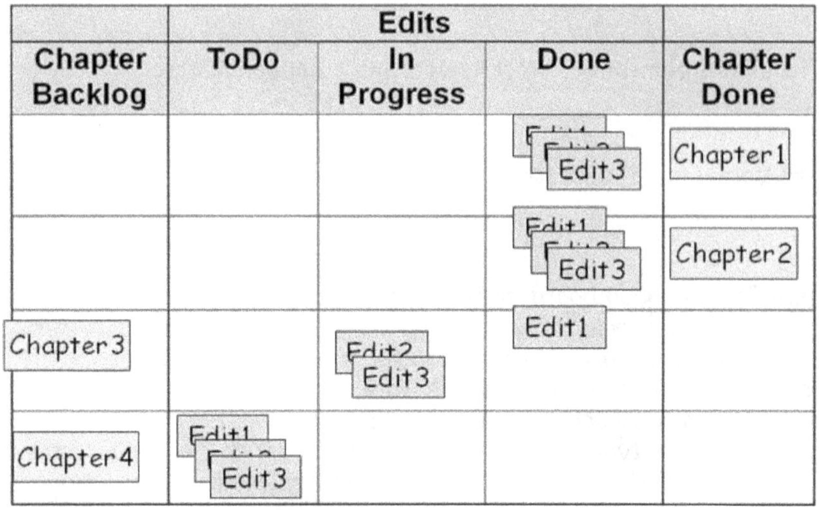

Chapter Backlog	Edits			Chapter Done
	ToDo	In Progress	Done	
			Edit1 Edit2 Edit3	Chapter 1
			Edit1 Edit2 Edit3	Chapter 2
Chapter 3		Edit2 Edit3	Edit1	
Chapter 4	Edit1 Edit2 Edit3			

Figure 1 - Classic XP-style task board.

PROBLEMS ENCOUNTERED

As I worked on subsequent chapters, I found additional things to do. Things like "make the voice consistent by changing all occurrences of 'You …' to 'We …'". This required adding additional edit stickies to my wall for each of the chapters. This was especially problematic for chapters that were already marked "Done," since now they had to be moved back to the Backlog column.Figure 2 - XP-Style task board with new edit task added *Figure 2 - XP-Style task board with new edit task added* shows the board after the new Edit 4 was added. Note how Chapters 1 and 2 are already marked "Done," yet they have a task outstanding.

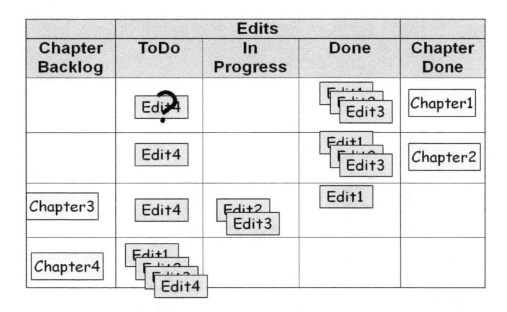

Chapter Backlog	Edits			Chapter Done
	ToDo	In Progress	Done	
	Edit4 (?)		Edit1 / Edit3	Chapter1
	Edit4		Edit1 / Edit3	Chapter2
Chapter3	Edit4	Edit2 / Edit3	Edit1	
Chapter4	Edit1 / Edit4			

Figure 2 - XP-Style task board with new edit task added

Also, there was no way to keep track of how much work remained because some edits applied to all chapters while others applied to just a few.

FINAL SOLUTION

The solution I ended up using was a matrix of Chapter vs. Edit. Each chapter was represented as a row in a spreadsheet. Each edit was represented as a column. The current status of the edit for the chapter was represented as both text and a color. (SeFigure 3-Column per edit with color-coded statuse *Figure 3 - Column per edit with color-coded status.*) Text was used to track the requirements of the step. "Yes" meant the work was required. "N/A" meant it was not needed. The cell could also contain specific notes if there was something particular to remember about it. Color was used to track the status. Blue fill with "Yes" meant it was not yet started. Green indicated the step was completed. Yellow indicated it was in progress. Note that there is no "Chapter Done" column anymore since the status of the chapter is implied from the status of the individual edits on the chapter.

Chapter	Edit.1	Edit.2	Edit.3	Edit.4
Narr.1	Done	Done	Done	Done
Narr.2	Done	Done	Done	Done
Narr.n	Done	Done		Yes
Smell.1	Yes	Yes	Yes	Yes
Smell.2	Yes	Yes	Yes	Yes
Smell.n	Yes	Yes	Yes	Yes
Pattern.1	Yes	Yes	Yes	Yes
Pattern.2	Yes	Yes	Yes	Yes
Pattern.n	Yes	Yes	Yes	Yes

Legend:

Yes	Needed
	In Progress
Done	Work done

Figure 3-Column per edit with color-coded status

Whenever I discovered a new edit to be applied to many or all chapters I would add a new column to the table. Initially, this column would be blank indicating "I don't know whether it applies to this chapter." (SFigure 4 - Color-coded status with newly added editee *Figure 4 - Color-coded status with newly added edit.*) As I worked on other tasks on a chapter, I would fill in this column as I noticed whether a newly added edit was required.

Chapter	Edit.1	Edit.2	Edit.3	Edit.4	Edit.5
Narr.1	Done	Done	Done	Done	
Narr.2	Done	Done	Done	Done	
Narr.n	Done	Done		Yes	
Smell.1	Yes	Yes	Yes	Yes	
Smell.2	Yes	Yes	Yes	Yes	
Smell.n	Yes	Yes	Yes	Yes	
Pattern.1	Yes	Yes	Yes	Yes	
Pattern.2	Yes	Yes	Yes	Yes	
Pattern.n	Yes	Yes	Yes	Yes	

Legend:

Yes	Needed
	In Progress
Done	Work done

Figure 4 - Color-coded status with newly added edit

Choosing Work

Whenever I finished something, I would update the color of the steps/chapters that I had just finished and then pick the next (set of) item(s) to work on. When the individual steps were small, I would typically pick a set of files to apply the same step to as shownFigure 5 - Same edit applied to several files at same time in *Figure 5 - Same edit applied to several files at same time.*

Chapter	Edit.1	Edit.2	Edit.3	Edit.n
Narr.1	Done	Done	Done	Done
Narr.2	Done	Done	Done	Done
Narr.n	Yes	Yes	Yes	Yes
Smell.1	Yes	Yes	Yes	Yes
Smell.2	Yes	Yes	Yes	Yes
Smell.n	Yes	Yes	Yes	Yes
Pattern.1	Yes		Yes	Yes
Pattern.2	Yes		Yes	Yes
Pattern.3	Yes		Yes	Yes

Figure 5 - Same edit applied to several files at same time

This would repeat until I had filled the entire column with green, at which point I would pick the next step. Some steps involved a lot more work (e.g. "Rewrite chapter 5 to ...") so I would do these one at a time and would start them when I felt fresh. When I was tired, or had only a short period of time available, I would focus on the more mechanical edits. When the edits were small enough that the overhead of opening the affected files was a large part of the effort (e.g. "Change all occurrences of 'we' to 'I'") I often chose several similar edits to do at the same time as showFigure 6 - Different edits applied to same file at same timen in Figure 6 - *Different edits applied to same file at same time*.

Chapter	Edit.1	Edit.2	Edit.3	Edit.n
Narr.1	Done	Done	Done	Done
Narr.2	Done	Done	Done	Done
Narr.n	Yes	Yes	Yes	Yes
Smell.1	Yes	Yes	Yes	Yes
Smell.2	Yes	Yes	Yes	Yes
Smell.n	Yes	Yes	Yes	Yes
Pattern.1				Yes
Pattern.2	Yes	Yes	Yes	Yes
Pattern.3	Yes	Yes	Yes	Yes

Figure 6 - Different edits applied to same file at same time

Managing WIP and Levelling Work

As this experience predated the publication of software-specific uses of Kanban, I did not explicitly model WIP limits on the Kanban matrix, but keeping WIP low was a key goal behind its use. The strategies I used for choosing the next batch of work implicitly kept WIP low because each batch consisted of a small set of Chapter(s)/Edit(s) intersections, and often it was a single edit applied to a single chapter. In fact, it was the desire to level the work by making the batches similar in duration — short enough to finish in a single sitting — that led to the use of the Kanban Matrix. The 100+ by 20+ matrix allowed a large degree of flexibility in choosing tasks that suited my time availability, energy level, and mood while maintaining a high level of discipline and making progress highly visible.

OTHER APPLICATIONS

I have used the Kanban Matrix on several other projects, including a systems integration project and a team-based book writing project.

Integration Project Management

We used a Kanban Matrix for visualizing and managing work when integrating SAP-based and PeopleSoft-based CRM functionality with an enterprise customer database as shoFigure 7 - Integration Project Architecture (some components omitted).

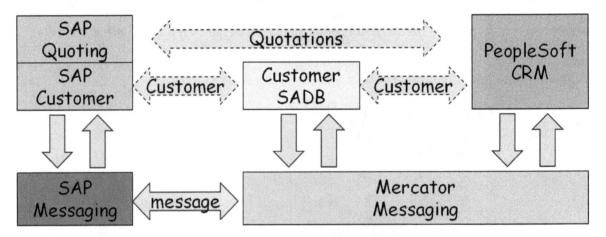

Figure 7 - Integration Project Architecture (some components omitted)

We decomposed each integration into stories per scenario and tasks representing various planning and development activities being done in parallel by the SAP, PeopleSoft, Enterprise Customer, and messaging-middleware resourcesFigure 8 - Waterfall workflow. See *Figure 8 - Waterfall workflow*. Each cell was colored in as the work was completed. Some resources worked story-by-story while others followed a traditional waterfall/BDUF approach. The matrix allowed the two approaches to be reconciled and managed.

Scenario	SAP HLD	CRM HLD	MOM HLD	SAP Coding	CRM Coding	MOD Coding	Integration Testing	Acceptance Testing
New Customer Req								
New Customer ACK								
New Customer NACK								
Edit Customer								
Edit Customer ACK								
New Quote								
Edit Quote								

Legend:
☐ In Progress
▨ Work done

Figure 8 - Waterfall workflow

Interestingly, when we first suggested a story-by-story approach, the ERP resources involved in the project all rejected the approach as impossible. At the insistence of the business sponsor they agreed to build a proof of concept by focusing initially on one integration scenario that including all the components. After this was built and demonstrated we were able to convince them to continue working scenario-by-scenario (as shFigure 9 - Incremental workflow with implicit WIP limitsown in *Figure 9 - Incremental workflow with implicit WIP limits*) rather than reverting to a waterfall approach.

Scenario	SAP HLD	CRM HLD	MOM HLD	SAP Coding	CRM Coding	MOD Coding	Integration Testing	Acceptance Testing
New Customer Req								
New Customer ACK								
New Customer NACK								
Edit Customer								
Edit Customer ACK								
New Quote								
Edit Quote								

Legend:
☐ In Progress
▨ Work done

Figure 9 - Incremental workflow with implicit WIP limits

The visibility provided to the business by the Kanban Matrix was a key motivator to adopt this approach. While we did not explicitly model WIP limits on this board, the board could easily be refactored to reflect the implicit WIP limits as sFigure 10 - Incremental workflow with explicit WIP limitshown in *Figure 10 - Incremental workflow with explicit WIP limits*. Integration testing was done by the development resources while acceptance testing was done by business resources.

Speciality:	SAP (1)		CRM (1)		MOM (1)		Integration Testing (1)	Acceptance Testing (1)
Scenario	HLD	Coding	HLD	Coding	HLD	Coding		
New Customer Req								
New Customer ACK								
New Customer NACK								
Edit Customer								
Edit Customer ACK								
New Quote								
Edit Quote								

Legend:
☐ In Progress
▨ Work done

Figure 10 - Incremental workflow with explicit WIP limits

Team-Based Book Writing Project

When I was asked to join a team at Microsoft Patterns & Practices writing a book on acceptance test engineering (Melnik, Meszaros 2011), we used a similar approach on a whiteboard wall to organize the work. Initially, the tasks were "Write first draft", "Peer Review First Draft", "Revise First Draft", and "PO (Product Owner) Review First Draft". Team members signed up for a particular task for each chapter/chunk. As the content matured, we evolved towards finer-grained tasks that were less of a workflow and more like the "kinds of things to do" described earlier. The matrix ended up being roughly 30 columns wide!

COMPARATIVE ANALYSIS

The Kanban Matrix represents largely the same information as a traditional Kanban board but it uses different visual clues, thereby avoiding some of the restrictions of the traditional board.

Workflow Definition

A traditional Kanban board uses a single token for the deliverable and uses columns to represent the different groups of workers between whom the work flows. This requires that there be an order in which the tasks/columns are carried out. The Kanban Matrix uses one row for each deliverable and columns for each task in the workflow regardless of who does the work. Therefore we may have many more columns than (types of) resources. In the personal book project, I had one column per task type even though there was only one resource (i.e. Me!) In the team-writing project, we also had one column per task type even though we had a pool of resources for some task types, while other tasks could only be done by our Product Owner. In the integration project, we had one column for each workflow phase (a macro task type) for each team (the resource type).

Tracking Progress

The traditional Kanban board uses movement of the token representing the deliverable between the columns as the indication of progress. Because there is a single token, this implies that only one column can be active at a time.

The Kanban Matrix indicates progress through a change of color. This allows many tasks to be "in progress" simultaneously for the same deliverable.

Backlog (To-do) and Work Completed (Done)

The traditional Kanban board only shows the deliverables being worked on and the next few deliverables "on deck". Availability of slots in the on deck column is often the trigger for the Product Owner to identify the next few deliverables, a process sometimes called "backlog grooming".

The Kanban Matrix shows all deliverables, including those to be done at some point in the future and those already completed. This allows the Kanban Matrix to act as a Release Burndown chart but in a format more akin to an FDD Parking Lot diagram (De Luca 2003) but it typically results in a much larger board. Filtering out the future and completed tasks dynamically (when using a tool or spreadsheet) can reduce it to a size more comparable to a traditional Kanban board.

Tools Support Required

Traditional Kanban boards are usually compact enough to represent on a physical wall chart. Movement of deliverables is accomplished by moving the card.

A Kanban Matrix is often too large to post on a physical board, and updating the colors of the cells is challenging when using felt markers. As a result, most Kanban Matrices I have used were stored electronically and reprinted when a physical board was desired. For usage by a single user, a simple spreadsheet may be all that is required. Cell coloring can be based on conditional formatting or done explicitly. For multiple users, the file locking problems associated with sharing a single document may be an issue. In these cases, a cloud-based shared spreadsheet such as Google Docs (Google 2011) may be preferable.

Limiting Work In Progress

Traditional Kanban boards indicate a limit on the number of items that can be in a particular state of the workflow by annotating a WIP limit on the corresponding column. The number of items in that state can be determined by counting the item cards in that column. The size of each deliverable is assumed to be similar enough that the WIP limits are relevant.

A Kanban Matrix does not assume that items in each column are of similar size. We can still annotate the columns with a WIP limit but it is less meaningful in that there is no assumption that particular columns would be done by the same resource(s). Instead, it makes more sense to apply WIP limits to a (team of) resource(Limiting Work in Progress-Progress in the next section.)

POSSIBLE ENHANCEMENTS

This report has thus far focused on actual experiences using a Kanban Matrix. The following are some ideas about how the Kanban Matrix could be enhanced to be more widely applicable.

Limiting Work in Progress

Since the Kanban Matrix doesn't assume that the work items are a similar size, it makes sense for a resource to aggregate several cells into a single "task". This makes tracking WIP difficult since we don't want to count each cell as having the same weight. One way this potential shortcoming could be avoided is to limit the total size (rather than number) of all the cells taken on by a particular resource or team. Each cell could have a numerical size estimate (as Figure 11 - Two teams pulling work based on own WIP limitsshown in *Figure 11 - Two teams pulling work based on own WIP limits*) and the WIP limit for a resource or team could limit the sum of these estimates that are selected and marked "in progress". When more than one heterogenious resource or team is pulling work from the same Kanban Matrix, we would need to mark the "in progress" cells with that team's in progress color or in progress pattern to be able to know how much work each team had in progress asFigure 11 - Two teams pulling work based on own WIP limits shown in *Figure 11 - Two teams pulling work based on own WIP limits*. Here, the Yellow team has a WIP limit of eight points and has taken on the first three items, totalling eight points in the row labelled "Pattern.1", while the Purple Team has taken on the third through fifth items in the column labelled "Edit.2", totalling nine points.

Chapter	Edit.1	Edit.2	Edit.3	Edit.n		Legend:		WIP Limit
Narr.1	Done	Done	Done	Done				
Narr.2	Done	Done	Done	Done		Legend:		Limit
Narr.n	1	∎3	3	2		TBD	Unknown (TBD)	
Smell.1	1	∎1	7	3		0	Not Needed	
Smell.2	1	∎2	5	2		2	Size: 2	
Smell.n	2	∎3	3	4			Yellow Team IP	8
Pattern.1	1	2	5	0		∎ ∎	Purple Team IP	10
Pattern.2	1	1	1	1		Done	Work done	
Pattern.3	2	2	7	2				

Figure 11 - Two teams pulling work based on own WIP limits

Hybridizing with Traditional Kanban Boards

Many of the benefits of the Kanban Matrix could be realized by combining them with traditional Kanban boards. For example, a single column in a traditional Kanban board could be replaced by a Kanban Matrix that breaks down the work into smaller pieces that could be done in parallel. When the card for the item moves into the matrix column, the status on the potentially parallel activities could be shown using color rather than card movement.

Development				Verification		Accept ed
(4) Todo	**(1) In Progress**			**(2) To Verify**	**(1) In Test**	
	HLD	Code1	Code2			
					Story 1	
		Story 2				
		Story 3				
Story 4						

CONCLUSION

The Kanban Matrix is a good way to visualize work when it is nonlinear. It allows individual steps to be done in any order and for some steps to be skipped altogether for some work items. When individual steps are very small, they can be aggregated into more manageable tasks easily.

One disadvantage is that it may make it harder to visualize the amount of work in progress simply because the progress of many more items can be tracked at the same time. These disadvantages might be overcome by merging Kanban Matrix concepts into more traditional Kanban board formats.

REFERENCES

Cohn, M. (2011). *Task Boards.* Training for Scrum Task Board use (website). Retrieved 14 March 2011 from http://www.mountaingoatsoftware.com/scrum/task-boards

De Luca, J. (2003). *Parking Lot Chart Example 1.* Feature Driven Development website. Retrieved 14 March 2011 from http://www.featuredrivendevelopment.com/node/630

Google (2011) http://spreadsheets.google.com

Melnik, G., and Meszaros, G. (2011). *Acceptance Test Engineering, Volume 1 – Thinking About Acceptance.* Redmond, WA: Microsoft Press

Meszaros, Gerard (2007). *xUnit Test Patterns – Refactoring Test Code.* Saddle River NJ: Addison-Wesley Professional

Gemba Walks and Visual Management

by

Inbar Oren, inbar@agilesparks.com

ABSTRACT

While Agile projects provide a lot of information, much of the information needed by managers still remains hidden. Moreover, many managers do not know what to look for and how to retain control in an Agile environment. Because of this, they usually either surrender control to the teams, losing the understanding of and sometimes the very essence of their job in the process, or they return to more known command and control patterns, hurting the teams. This article presents how Gemba walks can be used as a managerial tool when combined with visual management to help managers retain control, understanding, and a view of the big picture. This article explains where to walk, what to see, whom to talk to, and what to ask.

From this, managers should gain a new tool that will allow them to improve their own work and achieve understanding of where they can most effectively help the Agile teams, while preserving the team's autonomy.

THE VISIBILITY PROBLEM

When software groups move to Agile, there is usually an emphasis on allowing the teams to be self managed. This can be an abrupt shift if we use revolutionary frameworks such as Scrum, or a gradual change when we use evolutionary frameworks such as Kanban.

One of the main problems is that managers are left a little bit in the dark about their role. On the one hand, they might embrace the idea of self-managed teams, but on the other hand they want to retain some sort of control in order to be able to guide the teams. However, they lack the knowledge of how to do it in a self-managed context.

One of the hard things about being a manager in an Agile world is that while there might be a lot of information on the progress of projects, this information is at the same time visible and invisible.

It's visible because one cannot argue with the fact that, whether we use a physical board or an electronic tool, the information on what each team is doing is out there. The manager or any other interested party can simply walk up to the board or log-in to the tool and see what's going on.

The reason I say that this information is also invisible is because a manager who manages multiple teams, sometimes within one project, can find it hard to discern the big picture. In addition, since the self-managed Agile teams own the board, it is customized and built for their needs and not management's needs. This ownership of the team board is very important, especially in Kanban settings, but it detracts from the visibility.

Daily meetings are another great source of information, but with two problems: the manager might not have the time to visit daily meetings of all the teams he manages, and in Scrum at least, managers might not get the information they need since the daily is for the team and the manager cannot talk or ask questions.

It is, however, this kind of transparent and visual style of management which should give Agile development a lot of its strength. The sole question is this: How we can harness this visibility to the needs of the manager?

VISUAL PROJECT MANAGEMENT

If the team owns its own board, which should reflect the status of the team, the same applies to managers. Each manager and project manager should have her own board representing the status of her constituency.

This board is owned by the manager and reflects items which interest her and, just like an Agile team, should be able to look at the board and immediately see and understand her progress, so too should this board represent clearly and immediately the status of the entire project.

While the manager owns this wall, it should be centrally placed and highly visible to the Agile teams. They too want to see how their efforts tie into the bigger picture, and they also have responsibilities for this wall.

It is the team's responsibility to monitor this wall and reflect back to the manager its accuracy. Since the team members knows it progress better than anyone else, it should be left to them to make sure it reflects their progress as they see it.

It is important that these boards tell the story of the project or value stream by showing the overall status, but also should show a mini summary of the progress and problems of each station along its route.

Think of this board as something that tells a story, like an A3, or as a Dashboard which allows the manager and his superiors to quickly understand and see problems and wastes in the value stream.

Let me be clear; I see value in having a physical project board even if the company is using an electronic tool. While most of the information can come by printing reports from tools, one cannot get the full picture in one view on any decent type screen. I also see value in the fact that this board is constantly open and available to the manager, the teams, and other managers.

If the company has an amazing dash boarding tool that can present the status of the project or value stream on a single big screen, and such a screen is available and always turned to this dashboard, that is equally good. However, trusting people to login to tools to run reports and get a composite view of a project detracts from the clear visibility needed in an Agile environment.

THE GEMBA WALK

The Gemba is defined as "the place - any place in any organization - where humans create value" (Womack, xix). One of the central concepts of lean is the concept of the Gemba walk, a "tour" in which we "go see, ask why, show respect" (Womack, xix). The idea behind it is that managers of all levels should be present in the workplace, and understand problems by seeing them directly and talking to people who create value, not by staying in their office.

For me this is one of the most important aspects of Lean Management but, while in a physical plant the Gemba is a very clear place, and when you go there it is very clear what you see (though not always what to look for and what to ask), in software development the concept of the Gemba is more clouded.

We will try to answer five questions that will clarify how to do a Gemba walk in Software Development:

- Where does the manager go?
- What does she see?
- Whom does she talk to?
- What does she ask?
- How does she show respect?

Where to Go

So the first question should be where is the Gemba, and the answer, the real answer, is very simple: It is where developers code, testers test, technical writers write, business analysts analyze, and any other place where value is created along the value stream. And while I think managers should walk this route and visit people at their desks, I think that Gemba walks should provide more visibility than is available at the desks of everyone.

I think that the Gemba walk should focus on touring the visual boards of the value stream. Middle management should start each morning by walking along the value stream of each project. This tour group should include a representative of each station of the value stream, a person who will answer questions about his station.

The tour should end at the Project board and verify that it represents the entire status of the project as it is seen when walking the Gemba. There should then be a quick discussion on what is needed to proceed: are there stations we need to stop and fix? Are there stations working beyond their WIP limit? Should anything be escalated to upper management?

Upper management should perform a similar daily "tour'" of the various project boards, asking questions at each stop to make sure an even bigger picture (Release, Roadmap, etc.) progresses well.

It is important to walk the Gemba from downstream to upstream. This allows us to start as close as possible to the customer and understand how the problems downstream are caused by reasons upstream, and so understand the full story.

Once again, I think that having a physical always-on board of every team is critical; this can be a truly physical board or the electronic representation of one using any tool. I think that even if an electronic version is used several physical artifacts will be needed, but that is outside the scope of this article.

Since the board's point is to allow the team and any other interested parties to view the status of the team, having it hidden inside a tool is not true visibility. It also takes away responsibility from the team, as there is often one person updating the tool, and the rest never look at it. A lot of the time, if you ask the team members about their status they would refer you to the tool and have little or no direct knowledge of the answer. The investment in a large screen for the team board is, in my opinion, necessary.

This echoes Pascal Dennis' thoughts from "The remedy": "My questions elicit either blank stares or assurances that, 'It's in the computer.' That's what we used to say at NJMM. We've learned that the 'what's in the computer' is usually wrong." (Dennis, Kindle location 275) "It was a recurrent theme with business processes. Information was always in a box called the computer." (Dennis, Kindle location 2534) "Take information out of the box known as the computer and make it visible and understandable to users" (Dennis, Kindle location 3244). "Don't trust the computer screen, report, or phone message. Genchi genbutsu - Go see for yourself!" (Dennis, Kindle location 816)

We also want the place we visit to be physical place to avoid the temptation to do it in a room with a projector instead of actually walking the Gemba. Part of the benefit of doing a Gemba walk is to actually wander around the people; you will be surprised how much enthusiasm seeing management touring the board would instill in a team. You would likewise be surprised to see that as time progresses more team members come to their board to listen and answer questions. All these benefits would be lost if we stayed in a room and used a projector.

What to See
The thing to focus on in this Gemba walk is the big picture and how each board ties to it. We need to use this walk to identify a few things:

- Immediate problems - Immediate problems are things stopping each station from working. While these kinds of problems can and should be raised at the daily Gemba walk, if they are only raised then it indicates a problem. Immediate problems should be raised and handled as soon as they occur, and not wait for any daily meeting, be it the team's or the manager's. If this kind of problem does arise on a Gemba walk, it needs to get immediate attention in solving it. In addition, there needs to be a point Kaizen (a quick check of root causes to eliminate them), as well as a process Kaizen to see why it had to get to the manager's Gemba walk to be noticed and solved.

- Potential problems - One of the most important roles of the manager on her walk is to identify potential problems that either the team doesn't see yet or are coordination problems between teams.

- Kaizen opportunities - Another important thing to see are wastes in the process (too big or too small queues, defects, etc.), which can present opportunities to conduct Kaizen events or A3 analysis.

With Whom to Talk
As the idea is to walk the actual place where value is created, the people we need to talk to are the people actually creating the value. It is my recommendation that actual representatives from the team answer questions for the team at their station so that we can get the team's view.

The team representatives should join the entire tour so that they will connect to the entire value stream and achieve visibility beyond their specific station. The team representatives should also change periodically to expose more people to the value stream and to provide different views from within the team about their progress and problems.

What to Ask

While there cannot be a comprehensive list of questions to ask during the walk, I would like to give a few sample questions, which can explain how I see this walk.

1. What are the current problems at this station?
2. How is this station affected by stations upstream?
3. What problems could arise in the next few days?
4. Are WIP limits honored?
5. Are people working at a sustainable pace?

This is a short example of questions that can be asked. The important thing is to focus on immediate and potential problems. The manager needs to understand the flow of value along the project or value steam and any barriers or wastes in it.

It is also important to make sure that problems that occur are treated with a "stop and fix" mentality and that defects downstream are investigated upstream for root cause and counter measures.

The manager needs to make sure that problems are either handled immediately through point Kaizen, or have a problem owner that will handle them via A3 analysis.

To start this, the main question to ask is "why?" This focuses the team on researching root cause and on taking ownership for solutions.

How to Show Respect

A lot of people misunderstand respect. Respect is not letting people self-manage, giving them the task, and trusting them to do it. Rather, it is showing reciprocal respect between manager and team by asking difficult questions and engaging in conversations with the teams. This is more respectful, since it assumes that no one can do everything alone, and the manager is showing respect by allowing the team to tackle and solve the hard questions she poses.

CONCLUSION

While Agile teams should be self-managed and take ownership of their process, this does not mean that management should become distant from both the process and the execution.

Showing respect and allowing the teams to self-manage does not mean disappearing, much like giving the teams ownership does not reduce the responsibility of a manager to his project, team, or value stream.

In order to maintain the visibility needed by managers and to allow them to support the team as well as coach them, there is a need for managers to create their own boards, which showcase the status of the entire project or value stream.

There is also a need for managers to perform Gemba walks along the visibility boards of the different teams, following the value stream on its way up, to help themselves and the teams understand value stream-wide problems, and inter-station problems.

It is especially important to ask questions that will help those who provide value understand and solve their own problems and thus achieve an even greater level of self-management.

REFERENCES

Dennis, P. (2010). *The Remedy: Bringing Lean thinking out of the factory to transform the entire organization.* Hoboken, NJ: John Wiley & Sons.

Womack, J. (2011). *Gemba Walks.* Cambridge, MA: Lean Enterprise Institute.

Kanban in a CMMI ML3 Environment

by

Andrea Pinto, andrea.pinto@cesar.org.br

Felipe Furtado, felipe.furtado@cesar.org.br

ABSTRACT

Seeking a strategic positioning in the market for international software development, a Brazilian institute of innovation in information technology and communications has chosen to implement the CMMI level 3 in order to differentiate and improve the ability to execute its software projects. Beyond the necessity to define a process compliant to a maturity model, there was also an increasing motivation to use agile methodologies and get all the benefits associated with them: rapid response to market and change requests with high quality and productivity. In this context, Kanban started to be used in August 2009 in some software development projects at C.E.S.A.R (Recife Center for Advanced Studies and Systems). Currently it is being executed in a mobile software development internship program that has 27 intern software engineers. This paper describes the results reached using Kanban in a CMMI ML3 organization, especially in this internship program.

INTRODUCTION

In recent years, substantial changes have been happening in the software industry driven by market requirements. This scenario is demanding the attention of organizations to improve their software processes in the search for greater competitiveness and productivity. Accordingly, one of the organizations' challenges is to gain maturity in their development processes through the implementation of worldwide known quality models, as they are increasingly demanded by customers and used by competitors (SEI, 2006).

The CMMI (Capability Maturity Model Integration) provides a guide to improve the organization's process and its capacity to manage development, acquisition, and maintenance of products and services (Chrissis, 2007). The model defines a path to continuous improvement in terms of five levels of organizational maturity. Particularly at level 3, CMMI strengthens the control of project management in organizations, covering the areas of software engineering, process management, knowledge management, training, and formal decision making.

Seeking a strategic positioning in the market for international software development, a Brazilian institute of innovation in information technology and communications has chosen to implement the CMMI level 3 in order to differentiate and improve the ability to execute its software projects.

Beyond the necessity to define a process compliant to a maturity model, there was also an increasing motivation to use agile methodologies and get all the benefits associated with them: rapid response to market and change requests with high quality and productivity.

In this context, Kanban started to be used in August 2009 in some software development projects at C.E.S.A.R. (Recife Center for Advanced Studies and Systems). Currently it is being executed in a mobile software development internship program. We will show the results reached using Kanban in a CMMI ML3 organization.

PROCESS IMPROVEMENT WITH CMMI

One of the challenges faced by software development organizations is to acquire maturity in their development processes through the deployment of quality mature models globally recognized, seeing that they are more and more being required by clients and used by the competitors (SEI, 2006).

On the other hand, the market is imposing more competitive deadlines; to reach these deadlines the teams must be more agile and productive on the use of processes and identification of activities that do not add value to the final product (Boehm, 2006).

Thus, the challenge becomes even more complex, trying to achieve a maturity model without interfering with productivity, strongly based on the control of variables from a software development project, and at the same time adopting practices from agile projects.

The CMMI technical report (SEI, 2006) says that *"Only the statement of the specific or generic goal is a required model component."* (Fig. 1)

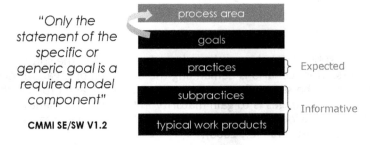

Figure 1. Achieving a CMMI Maturity Level (SEI, 2006).

Organizations that have a defined process, where the software development phases and activities are described, generally need to tailor the defined process to adapt it considering the projects' scope. It is necessary to define an instance of the defined process to attend the project needs so that is adherent to the organizational process (SEI, 1994).

Figure 2 shows the evolution of a software development process, called ProSCes, which already has 11 years of existence. Initially it was defined based on Rational Unified Process (RUP) and Project Management Body of Knowledge (PMBOK). In 2003, the process was improved and assessed SW-CMM N2. In 2004 C.E.S.A.R went through a certification of ISO 9001, but was more focused on the company's internal processes. Before CMMI L3 evaluation, which occurred in 2007, the company began to experiment with agile methodologies.

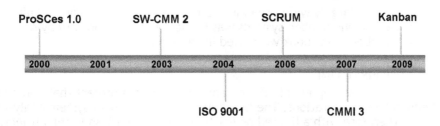

Figure 2. Organizational Development Process Evolution (http://www.cesar.org.br)

Therefore, Scrum was chosen as the first agile methodology to be introduced into CMMI level 3 compliant processes. This resulted in a process with an agile and adaptable core, which is light in comparison with the traditional CMMI approach (SEI, 2006) that includes a formal quality mechanism to encourage the culture of continuous progress.

To achieve the compatibility of the CMMI with agile methodologies it was necessary to understand the components of CMMI, requiring further studies related to iterations, teams' behavior, other methodologies, and project life cycle, among other things. CMMI prescribes that a software process must be defined and executed, but does not determine how it should be implemented in the organization.

Kanban has been used since 2009, as will be detailed in the following sections. To guide how the tailoring must be made in the project context, the organizational process should include the criteria for adaptation. The definition of criteria for the organizational process is an activity that requires a deep understanding of the types of applications developed in the organization in order to provide opportunities and reduce the effort to modify the process definition (Xu, 2005).

Within this context, this experience report presents how a mature development process can be improved and simplified to become more compatible with agile principles.

LEAN AND KANBAN

Most of the activities executed in software projects (tests just at the end of the project, elaboration of unnecessary documents, etc.) cause the wasting of time and energy for the development teams and do not add value to the final product. Lean has emerged at Toyota after World War II with the goal of increasing the production efficiency by the continuous cutting out of waste (Poppendieck and Poppendieck, 2003).

Lean has also emerged to promote a huge impact in productivity based on the idea that the productivity will increase if we stop doing anything that is not going to be directly related with the value for which the client will pay. This is the main concept of Lean: stop doing things that do not add value to the client. These things are called waste. Lean turns our attention to a quick, regular, and quality flow, without working on unnecessary activities and with no defects (Poppendieck and Poppendieck, 2003).

Many tools and techniques were developed to allow the organizations to apply the Lean concepts and ideas. Many of them have emerged from TPS (Toyota Product System): Kanban, JIT (Just In Time), Jidoka, kaizen, etc. Kanban is a Japanese technique integrated to the JIT concept that was born in Toyota and is largely widespread in the inventory production and administration fields. The concept of Kanban and Kanban systems was brought to the IT industry by Anderson (2010). The concepts described in his book were used in this work.

KANBAN IN USE FOR THE FIRST TIME

The first time Kanban was applied in the organization was in a project that had already started and had been divided in iterations. The first author was the project system analyst with partial allocation, and therefore with a limited power to implement Kanban in the project. Still, efforts were made in this sense. The client provided us a general requirements specification with the prioritization and distribution of the requirements in each one of the iterations. There were four iterations with a one-month duration each. The organization already had a CMMI ML3 process that was tailored to the project to attend some specific needs as the activities related to user centered design and use of Kanban. We started using Kanban in the project as a pilot with the goal of evaluating the use of the framework in software development projects where the software development process is well defined and adherent to CMMI ML3. The macro development process activities executed in each one of the iterations were the following:

1. Requirements detailing with the client;

2. Elaboration of a low fidelity prototype using the Balsamiq tool;

3. Execution of usability tests with potential users using the low fidelity prototypes;

4. Requirements reworking considering the results of the usability tests as well as the test cases specification elaborated in parallel;

5. Application screens design;

6. Requirements development;

7. Bug fixes related to the internal baselines and prior releases.

There were weekly baselines that were planned at the beginning of each iteration. Steps 1 to 4 were executed by the system analyst, designer, and UX researcher.

As the team members did not know the Kanban framework (only the system analyst and team leaders knew it), and to smoothly introduce the Kanban concepts, the first version of the Kanban board had only four columns: Requirements, Analysis, Development, and Defects (at this time we did not know how to deal with defects) with a swimlane for each one of the requirements.

In the Requirements column there were the requirements of the current iteration identified using a post-it with its ID and Name; the requirements were specified using an internal requirements management tool (Furtado et al., 2010). The Analysis column was used to work in the following activities: requirements specification, prototype elaboration, screens design, and test cases specification. When all the activities were finished the Development activity was initiated. In the Defect column the testers included the defects found in the baselines.

The number of activities that could be pulled to a column (WIP - Work-In-Progress) considered the quantity of team members and the number of activities being executed in the column. Each team member received three avatars, but the use of the third avatar was discouraged.

The first Kanban board (Fig. 3) was designed by the system analyst and team leader, putting in the Requirements column the requirements that would be developed in the current iteration. This was done despite the fact that Kanban does not use iterations, but as the project was planned in this way, we chose not change this in order to avoid misunderstandings with the client.

Figure 3. The First Kanban Board.

The Kanban board was improved after two iterations and the second version had five more columns: three buffer columns used to list the activities that were finished but could not be pulled to the next column, one Test column, and one Release column, where we included the requirements ready to be delivered to the client.

In this first use of Kanban we learned a lot. We could better understand the Kanban concepts like WIP, we proved that it is possible to use allocation Kanban in a software development project where the software process was adherent to CMMI ML3, and we understood the use of work types, as in the second version of the board we had the expedited items and defects treated as a work type.

Kanban Used in another Context
Currently Kanban is being used in a software development internship program (Fig. 4). The program duration is seven months, where the 27 intern software engineers have the responsibility to develop at least 54 applications while also having classes to learn the programming language. The 27 intern software engineers were divided in three teams, each one with a technical leader, a designer, and a UX researcher. Besides that, the whole team has a team leader, a technical team leader, and one project manager partially allocated. Kanban in this context helped to allocate the applications between the teams considering team capacity and productivity.

The Kanban system was designed considering the value stream of the applications development from the moment a team member (usually the technical leader) pulls an application "idea" to development until the application is delivered for client test acceptance. During the workflow all the team members were involved in the process at any given time. This was represented through smaller post-its on top of the application post-it identifying each one of the roles: green post-its for testers, blue post-its for UX (User Experience) and designers, and yellow post-its for intern software engineers. The WIP was limited in the workflow steps and the lead time was measured. The applications were delivered when they were ready for client test acceptance, but no specific delivery dates were defined with the client. There were what we called internal due dates as an additional tool to guarantee team focus.

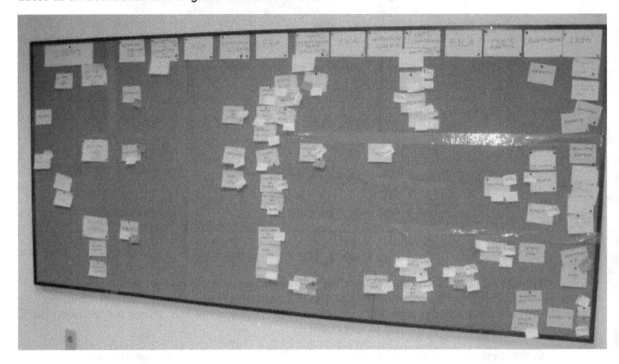

Figure 4. The Current Kanban Board.

The value stream started when the ideas for new applications were approved by the client; each one of the approved ideas was represented with an orange post-it on the leftmost column. Then the ideas could be pulled by anyone on the team. The board was divided in three swimlanes, each one representing a team; this was made only to easily track the progress of each team. The next column on the board showed the ideas that were pulled by each one of the teams.

Then we have the *Pesquisa de Similar* (Benchmarking) as the first activity in the workflow. During this activity the UX researcher would look for similar ideas in other mobile platform stores with the goal of suggesting innovative differentials for the application that was to be developed.

After that, the UX researcher elaborated the application wireframe, showing the application's main functionalities and the navigational model, and the designer would elaborate two or three options for the application visual esthetic; in this activity — named Estética/Protótipo/Fluxo

(Estethic/Prototype/Flow - navigational model) — the UX researcher and the designer elaborated a document that should be sent for client approval. When the document was finished the UX researcher or designer pulled the post-it to next column board (a queue). When we had a certain number of ideas ready to be sent for the client (usually three or four) the post-its would be pulled to the Aprovação do Cliente (Client Approval) queue; we had the visibility of which ideas were in the client's hands waiting for approval.

When the client approved the document the post-it would be pulled to the next queue, where the ideas waited to be pulled by a designer who would work on the application layout proposal, considering the esthetic approved by the client. The designer should elaborate another document with the images created for the application, usually the main screen, another relevant screen chosen by the designer with the help of other team members, and the application's icon. After some ideas had their design proposal ready — they waited in a queue — they were sent for client approval. This was the second and last interaction with the client until the application was released.

Then the application was pulled to the Development column where the intern software engineers were responsible to implement it, the designer was responsible to finish all the application design (screens, buttons, images), the UX researcher was responsible to give support to the team with the application usability, and the testers were responsible to write the test cases. After development the tests were executed, and when all the defects were corrected the application was released to client acceptance.

The system process design worked very well, stimulating team members to self management. Suggestions were usually made such as, "I can see on the board that the wireframes of team X are a little late, don't you think is a good idea if I help the team?" or "I can see that we have finished the design of our applications' team, may I help team Y to accomplish design of application A that I am familiar with the visual esthetic chosen?" Also, the intern software engineers that got engaged in the use of the cardboard could see what applications were being finished and were free to choose what applications they would like to work on next.

The lead time of the applications development was measured since the cardboard data was collected daily during the project execution. Figure 5 shows the daily collected data considering the workflow phases. As data began to be collected when the project was already ongoing, the chart shows activities being executed in all phases since the first days.

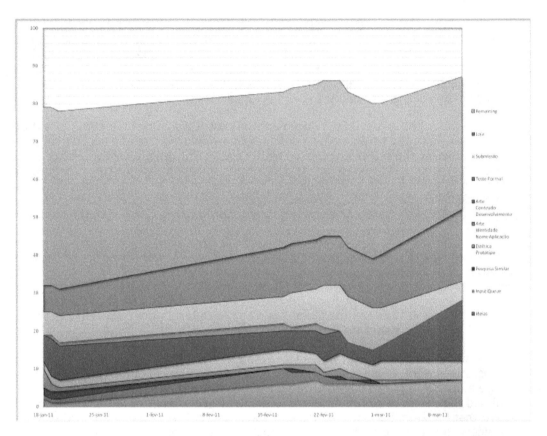

Figure 5. Chart with data daily collected from the card board.

CONCLUSION

The transition to Kanban in a CMMI ML3 organization was made smoothly and brought us great results, mainly related to workflow visibility. The workflow visibility helped the team's self management, diminishing the work of the team leader, since the team was large (36 team members) and helped also to easily view the workflow bottlenecks. In this project the quantity of designers was underestimated; we started the project with three designers and after four months the number was increased by three. We also had to subcontract the design of some applications since we did not have capacity to do it. However, all the necessary changes were made with transparency with the client, since we had weekly meetings where applications' statuses were shown. We also had a spreadsheet with the workflow and applications that was updated weekly.

We had also, for the first time in this kind of project, the real visibility of the lead time. We know how much time is necessary to develop a mobile application in an internship software development program where the intern software engineers are learning to use the development platform and are immature in the software development process.

REFERENCES

Anderson, D.(2010). *Kanban – Successful Evolutionary Change for Your Technology Business*. Sequim, WA: Blue Hole Press.

Balsamiq (2011). http://balsamiq.com/.

Boehm B. (2006) *"A View of 20th and 21st Century Software Engineering"*, 2006 International Conference on Software Engineering.

Chrissis B., Korad, M. & Shrum, S. (2007). *CMMI Guidelines for Process Integration and Product Improvement*, Second Edition, Addison-Wesley, EUA.

Furtado, F. Pinto, A., Carvalho, G., Albuquerque, R. (2010). *"Customização e Integração de Ferramentas Open-Source. Uso de ferramentas integradas para melhoria de processo e aumento de produtividade"*, Engenharia de Software Magazine. http://www.devmedia. com.br/articles/viewcomp.asp?comp=15775.

Poppendieck, M., Poppendieck, T.(2003). *"Lean Software Development: An Agile Toolkit"*, Boston, MA: Addison-Wesley.

SEI. (1994). *"Process Tailoring and the Software Capability Maturity Model"*. http://www.sei. cmu.edu/pub/documents/94.reports/pdf/tr24.94.pdf, CMU/SEI-1994-TR24.

SEI. (2006). *"CMMI for Development, version 1.2, staged representation"*. CMU/SEI-2006-TR-008 from http://www.sei.cmu.edu/pub/documents/06.reports/pdf/06tr008.pdf.

Xu, Peng. (2005). *"Knowledge Support in Software Process Tailoring"*. Proceedings of the 38th Hawaii International Conference on System Sciences.

Boyd's OODA Loop: Not What You Think

by

Chet Richards, crichards@jaddams.com

ABSTRACT

Although the strategic ideas of John Boyd encompass much more than the well known "OODA loop," the loop does provide a concise framework for improving competitive power throughout an organization. However, much of this power will be lost if people use the most common version of the loop. Fortunately, Boyd only drew one sketch of the OODA loop, and that version is the key to his entire body of work. This paper reviews the research on Boyd's concept of the OODA loop, indicates parallels between the concept and lean practices, and suggests ways to use Boyd's actual version to improve business strategy and operations.

CREATING STRATEGY

The late USAF Colonel John R. Boyd (1927-1997) was hard on ideologues: "Don't be a member of Clausewitz's school because a lot has happened since 1832," he would warn his audiences, "and don't be a member of Sun Tzu's school because an awful lot has happened since 400 BC."

By implication, we should not be members of Boyd's school, either: "If you're going to regard this stuff as dogma," he would say at some point in his briefings, "you'd be better served to take it out and burn it." Why, then, spend time studying his works today? Boyd's (1987a) answer was to follow his own example, to examine a variety of approaches, "domains" he termed them, take what is useful from each, and by testing in the real world, evolve strategies accordingly.

Boyd Lives!

Individuals and organizations that adopt this approach to life can create their own schools of great power and influence (Boyd, 1992). In his eulogy, General Charles Krulak (as cited in Osinga, 2005, p. 1), a former commandant of the U.S. Marine Corps and confidant of Boyd, summarized his influence on military strategy:

> The Iraqi army collapsed morally and intellectually under the onslaught of American and Coalition forces. John Boyd was an architect of that victory as surely as if he'd commanded a fighter wing or a maneuver division in the desert. His thinking, his theories, his larger than life influence, were there with us in Desert Storm. He must have been proud of what his efforts wrought.

Osinga (2005) noted that beyond the foundational outline of the maneuver warfare doctrine used by the Marine Corps in the 2003 Gulf War, Boyd's influence reached deep into the theory of conflict. Such as ideas like agility, shaping the mind of the enemy, harmony among all levels, and perhaps most important of all, promoting, not just exploiting or responding to, uncertainty and disorder, "were all either invented, re-discovered or inspired by Boyd." (p. 4). In his work, Osinga concluded that:

> Reading through Boyd's work nowadays one does not encounter novelty or experience difficulty following his arguments and accepting his ideas. His language and logic, his ideas, terms and concepts are part and parcel now of the military conceptual frame of reference. Western military organizations have to a large extent internalized Boyd's concepts, and perhaps even learned Boyd's way of thinking. (p. 316)

Nissestad (2007) summarized Boyd's contributions to modern strategy, and particularly to its leadership component, as:

> Boyd was the first in the modern era, to propose a comprehensive theory of strategy that is independent of size or technology and to identify an organizational climate for achieving it. (p. 11)

> (Boyd) was the first to observe that the common underlying mechanism involved tactics that distort the enemy's perception of time. He identified a general category of activities to achieve this distortion, the ability to change the situation faster than the opponent could comprehend, which he called "operating inside the Observation-Orientation-Decision-Action (OODA) loop." (pp. 11-12)

> Boyd was not the first to appreciate initiative, even by privates and sailors, but he was the first to tie a specific climate based on initiative to the ability to generate rapid transients in combat and other conflicts. (p. 12)

Prior to his career as a strategist, Boyd exercised a profound influence on the design of air-to-air fighter aircraft and the tactics used to employ them. He was the first to quantify a method of assessing the relative merits of two such aircraft across their entire flight envelopes, a method that is taught to fighter pilots to this day as "energy-maneuverability." Perhaps the best known aircraft designed according to Boyd is the F-16, which Boyd also helped select as the winner of a competition in 1975 and is still in production (Coram, 2002; Hammond, 2001; Osinga, 2005).

Finally, at the end of his life, after the fall of the Soviet Union, he turned his attention away from war towards other forms of conflict, including business. Tom Peters referred to Boyd twice in his last major work, *Re-imagine!* (2003) and Boyd was an inspiration for Peters' breakaway strategy book, *Thriving on Chaos* (Osinga 2005; Richards 2004). Although Boyd did not write on business per se he did collaborate with me on my book, *Certain to Win* (Coram, 2002; Richards, 2004), which drew parallels between Boyd's concepts of maneuver conflict and the principles underlying lean philosophies.

Boyd himself might have lost interest in armed conflict, but his influence on our national defense debate lives on. The American Secretary of Defense, Robert M. Gates (2010), summarized Boyd's contributions in an address to cadets at the U.S. Air Force Academy in Colorado Springs in April 2010:

> As a 30-year-old captain, he rewrote the manual for air-to-air combat and earned

the nickname "40-second" Boyd for the time it took him to win a dogfight. Boyd and the reformers he inspired would later go on to design and advocate for the F-16 and the A-10. After retiring, he developed the principals (sic) of maneuver warfare that were credited by a former Marine Corps commandant and a secretary of defense for the lightning victory of the first Gulf War.

The OODA loop

If people know anything about Boyd, it has something to do with the OODA loop (Osinga, 2005). The acronym OODA stands for "observe, orient, decide, act," and it is often depicted with the four elements arranged in a simple sequence, as if the acronym stood for "observe, then orient, then decide, then act," as shown in Figure 1 (Osinga, 2005; Richards, 2004).

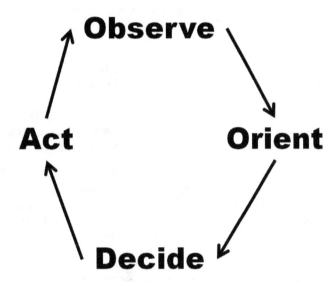

Figure 1. The OODA loop is often depicted as a simple sequential process.

Osinga (2005) described the usual interpretation of the OODA loop as a tool for strategy:

> In the popularized interpretation, the OODA loop suggests that success in war depends on the ability to out-pace and out-think the opponent, or put differently, on the ability to go through the OODA cycle more rapidly than the opponent. Boyd's name will probably always remain associated with the OODA loop and this popular interpretation. (p. 6)

Thus the study of conflict is reduced to "dueling OODA loops," with the side that can go through its loop more quickly building an insurmountable competitive advantage. An important corollary to this approach is that the side that can make the quickest decisions is most likely to win (Osinga, 2005).

As simple and beguiling as this conception might be, it is not a powerful weapon of strategy, either in war or for business. There are several reasons for this possibly counterintuitive conclusion:

- The most important is that the concept of a simple, sequential loop does not model well how organizations in conflict act. A British officer, Jim Storr (Osinga, 2005) summarized this situation:

    The OODA process is not circular. It apparently takes 24 hours to execute a divisional operation. Planning takes a minimum of 12 hours. Thus a divisional OODA loop would have to be at least 36 hours long. Yet the Gulf War and other recent operations show divisions reacting far faster. Military forces do not in practice wait to observe until they have acted. Observation, orientation and action are continuous processes, and decisions are made occasionally in consequences of them. There is no OODA loop. The idea of getting inside the enemy decision cycle is deeply flawed. (p. 8)

- In the circular version, speed of decision and quality of decision can trade off. In war, however, great commanders have sometimes found it advantageous to take extra time making a decision in order to incorporate more complete intelligence and reach a better understanding of the situation. This is especially true of the types of unconventional warfare that developed countries are confronting today and which often go under the name "protracted war" (Hammes, 2004).

- Similarly in business: One of the earliest papers on the Toyota Development System carried the subtitle, "How delaying decisions can make better cars faster" (Ward, Liker, Cristiano, & Sobeck, 1995). The authors of that paper noted that a company can minimize the total design time of a car not by making decisions more quickly than its competitors but by ensuring that decisions, once made, never need to be revisited.

With objections as serious as these, it is good that Boyd never drew the OODA "loop" as depicted in Figure 1, nor did he ever describe it as a sequential process in any of his works on competitive strategy.

THE REAL OODA "LOOP"
For his Ph.D. dissertation on Boyd, Dutch fighter pilot Colonel Frans Osinga (2005) took the concept of "rapid OODA looping" head on. His thesis was, "Boyd's OODA loop concept as well as his entire work is more comprehensive, deeper and richer than the popular notion of 'rapid OODA looping' his work is generally equated with" (p. 10). He did not discredit the concept of the OODA loop but made the case that the power of Boyd's ideas comes from using the right one, the "loop" that Boyd actually drew.

Why an OODA Loop?
In his presentations on armed conflict — war — Boyd never wrote the term "OODA loop" alone but used the phrase "operating inside opponents' OODA loops," which he was careful to never define explicitly. The closest he came was 132 charts into his major briefing on war, *Pat-*

terns of Conflict (Boyd, 1986) where he stated that to operate inside an adversary's OODA loop was to "Observe, orient, decide and act more inconspicuously, more quickly, and with more irregularity ..." This was considerably more than "observe, then orient, then decide, then act." He made the claim that the ability to perform this more sophisticated version enabled one to execute a list of heinous acts upon one's adversary, ending with "Generate uncertainty, confusion, disorder, panic, chaos ... to shatter cohesion, produce paralysis and bring about collapse."

But what about the OODA loop itself, as contrasted with "operating inside the OODA loop"? Boyd (1996) made even more expansive claims for it:

> Without OODA loops, we can neither sense, hence observe, thereby collect a variety of information for the above processes, nor decide as well as implement actions in accord with these processes. (p. 2)

When combined with the idea of operating inside adversary's OODA loops, the OODA loop provided the key to success not just in war but in life itself:

> Without OODA loops embracing all of the above and without the ability to get inside other OODA loops (or other environments), we will find it impossible to comprehend, shape, adapt to and in turn be shaped by an unfolding evolving reality that is uncertain, everchanging, and unpredictable. (p. 2)

In contrast to the concept of "operating inside the OODA loop," however, Boyd not only defined the OODA loop itself, but drew a picture (Figure 2), and it is safe to say it was not what most people expected.

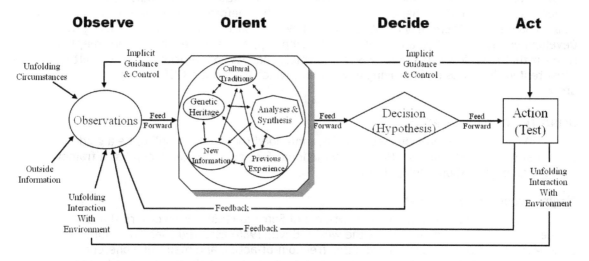

Figure 2. The only OODA "loop" that Boyd actually drew.

Interpreting the OODA "Loop" Sketch

The "loop" depicted in Figure 2 is a wonderful framework for strategy, but it can appear complex at first. To get a handle on it, begin with the centrality of orientation, with action flowing implicitly from it most of the time. This puts the focus on maintaining awareness of what is going on in the world, including ourselves, and ensuring that our understanding is always better than that of any competitor. Orientation is an ancient idea, embodied in the concept of mindfulness, but it is as modern as fighter pilots, who talk about maintaining "situation awareness."

What this focus on orientation does is make conflict into a learning contest to better maintain awareness of the world, as it is of, as Collins (2001) called it, "brutal reality." But success under this model is not a simple, accumulative process, where one gradually adds to one's net competitive advantage account. The purpose of all this awareness is to be able to act, particularly in the style known as "asymmetric fast transients" or "cheng/ch'i." (Boyd, 1986; Gimian & Boyce, 2008)

The basic pattern is simple: An organization uses its better understanding (clearer awareness) of the unfolding situation to set up its opponent by employing actions that fit in with the opponent's expectations, which Boyd, following Sun Tzu (1988), called the *cheng*. When the organization senses (via its previous experiences, including training) that the time is ripe, it springs the *ch'i*, the unexpected, extremely rapidly (Gimian & Boyce, 2008). Musashi (1982) concluded that this will produce a period, though perhaps only a moment, of confusion, hesitation, surprise, even debilitating shock and disorientation that Japanese strategists call a *suki*. During that period, when the opponent does not have an accurate understanding of the situation, we can act with little fear of effective counter-actions by our opponents.

Time becomes a critical factor because we need to act when we intend to act. Boyd (1987b) concluded that at times, such as exploiting a breakthrough, this may be at a very rapid tempo — cheng/ch'i after cheng/ch'i after cheng/ch'i — before the opponent can understand what is happening. There may be other times, however, such as designing a car using the Toyota Development System, when an organization's tempo appears slow, even cumbersome, but the end result is that it achieves its objectives more rapidly than its competition. Such a result is entirely consistent with a focus on improving orientation, which is with the OODA "loop" depicted in Figure 2.

USING THE OODA "LOOP"

As noted in the previous section, Boyd intended the OODA "loop" to be a guide for actions that will achieve success. Here are some ideas for employing the "loop" as a framework to improve an organization's competitive power.

Singing From the Same Sheet

The first, following the ancient wisdom of Sun Tzu (1988), is to ensure that everyone on the team shares a similar view of the world. Boyd (1986) asserted that "Without a common outlook superiors cannot give subordinates freedom-of-action and maintain coherency of ongoing action." Therefore, "A common outlook ... represents a unifying theme that can be used to simultaneously encourage subordinate initiative yet realize superior intent" (p. 74). Boyd illustrated this in Figure 2, where the individual orientation blocks should be sufficiently similar that they roughly align into this common outlook. It is this alignment that allows for the cheng/ch'i style of action described earlier.

In employing this concept, consider four elements: the orientations that people bring into the organization, their initial training and indoctrination in the organization, experiences in the groups where they work, and their knowledge of the brutal reality of the current situation.

Brutal Reality

This last point bears some emphasis. Essentially it requires leaders to take action to ensure that their (similar implicit) orientation is at all times more accurate than any competitors'.

Because accuracy spoils quickly, however, better awareness is primarily a function of interaction with the environment, both internal and external. Information must be infused throughout the organization to help keep everybody's orientations generally aligned. Boyd considered the requirement to assess (he used the term "appreciate") the depth of common understanding in an organization to be one of the primary functions of leadership (1987a).

Navel-gazing

Boyd's advice on this subject is "Don't." The OODA "loop" is firmly grounded in actions, things that organizations do to shape and, if necessary, react to the environment. Excellence in whatever repertoire of actions the organization chooses to have is vitally important if it is to honor promises to customers and avoid consequences of poor actions such as the delays and cost overruns that have recently bedeviled the commercial aircraft industry.

The OODA "loop" suggests that a good way to mitigate this problem is to wire the repertoire to Orientation via the "implicit guidance and control" link. That is, most of the time, action should flow from Orientation without detailed, explicit instructions. Boyd (1987a) insisted that "The key idea is to emphasize implicit over explicit in order to gain a favorable mismatch in friction and time (i.e, ours lower than any adversary) for superiority in shaping and adapting to circumstances" (p. 22).

Because the ability to operate via the implicit guidance and control link played such a fundamental role in Boyd's strategy, he examined it to some extent in all of his major briefings, particularly on pages 22ff. of *Organic Design* (1987a) and page 74 of *Patterns of Conflict* (1986). Vandergriff (2006) and the Royal Norwegian Naval Academy (2009) have developed methods for building this ability in junior military officers, and leaders in other fields may find their methods applicable to their organizations.

It is not enough, though, to achieve ever greater degrees of excellence in a specified collection of tasks. Organizations that take this approach make themselves vulnerable to competitors who can predict these increasingly predictable actions and create new ways to counter them. Oddly, the process for evolving new actions does involve a generally circular process (reminiscent of Figure 1) of observe, then orient, then decide, then act, as indicated by the "decision" and "test" captions in Figure 2 and by the well-known PDCA cycle. As Boyd (1992) made clear, however, these circular processes perform the functions of science, technology, and engineering, where there is no thinking and malevolent adversary. They create the tools that strategy and tactics then employ, via the full power of Figure 2.

Your Repertoire

By making the above the focus of attention, leaders can create and evolve practices that will improve their competitive abilities. Here are some ideas:

- Establish a college. General Electric has Crotonville, 19th century Germany had the famous *Kriegsakademie*, and most militaries today have an array of staff and war colleges. These build skills and in the process provide a common foundation (which the military calls "doctrine") on which to inculcate the similar implicit orientation required by the OODA loop.

- Give your human resources department a real mission, other than just pushing papers and acting as bureaucratic police. The best mission might be as keeper of the culture, but without a day-to-day line management role (Welch, J. & Welch, S., 2005). Consider recruiting from line management as a special tour of duty for high potentials: They operate in the culture, and then they get to step back and think about the culture, perhaps in conjunction with the college you established in the previous bullet.

There are other possibilities. Family businesses, for example, have the unique advantage of being able to use non-employee family members for this role (Astrachan, Richards, Marshisio & Manners, 2010).

For the specifics of a competitive culture, Boyd (1986) suggested an "organizational climate," characterized largely by the four German words described in *Certain to Win* (Richards, 2004). The most important attribute to this organizational climate is that it fosters creativity and initiative throughout the organization (Nissestad, 2007). Your team should investigate, make your own decisions, and document them in an organizational doctrine document.

Write and nurture a living "doctrine manual" as the explicit component of an organization's culture. Think of this not as a checklist or menu that must be followed (or else!) but as "standard work" in the language of the Toyota Way (Liker, 2004). As Ohno (1988) insists, it is of critical importance that the people performing the work write the standard work document themselves. Given its importance to the organization, you might consider a contribution to the manual to be a prerequisite for promotion to senior levels.

All of the above is interesting but falls firmly into the category of navel-gazing unless it results in verifiable actions. As one of my colleagues at Kennesaw State University often puts it, "Can you demonstrate the claim you just made? Data would be nice." (G. E. Manners, personal communication, January 15, 2009). For example, can you demonstrate that our orientation is more accurate than any of our competitors'? That is, what makes you think that it is, and can you convince anyone else? You can apply this simple test to all of the recommendations that Boyd made, and senior management must create an environment where people enjoy and take pride in doing so.

CONCLUSION

Boyd's OODA "loop" provides an effective framework for aligning and focusing the efforts of leaders throughout an organization to improve their organization's competitive abilities. For the "loop" to work, however, organizations must use the one Boyd actually drew and create their own practices suitable for their people and their competitive environments.

REFERENCES

Astrachan, J. H., Richards, C. W., Marchisio, G. G., & Manners, G. E. (2010). The OODA loop: A new strategic management approach for family business. In P. Mazzola & F. W. Kellermans (Eds.), *Handbook of research on strategy process* (pp. 541-566). Cheltenham (UK): Edward Elgar.

Boyd, J. R. (1986). *Patterns of conflict.* (Unpublished briefing). Retrieved from http://dnipogo.org/john-r-boyd/

Boyd, J. R. (1987). *Organic design for command and control.* (Unpublished briefing). Retrieved from http://dnipogo.org/john-r-boyd/

Boyd, J. R. (1987). *Strategic game of ? and ?* (Unpublished briefing.) Retrieved from http://dnipogo.org/john-r-boyd/

Boyd, J. R. (1992). *Conceptual spiral.* (Unpublished briefing). Retrieved from http://dnipogo.org/john-r-boyd/

Boyd, J. R. (1996). *The essence of winning and losing.* (Unpublished briefing). Retrieved from http://dnipogo.org/john-r-boyd/

Collins, J. (2001). *Good to great: Why some companies make the leap... and others don't.* New York, NY: HarperCollins.

Coram, R. (2002). *Boyd: The fighter pilot who changed the art of war.* New York, NY: Little Brown.

Gates, R. M. (2010). United States Air Force Academy Lecture (Leadership/Character). Retrieved from http://www.defense.gov/Speeches/Speech.aspx?SpeechID=1443

Gimian, J. & Boyce B. (2008). *The rules of victory: How to transform chaos and conflict.* Boston, MA: Shambhala.

Hammes, T.X. (2004). *The sling and the stone: On war in the 21st century.* St. Paul, MN: Zenith.

Hammond, G. T. (2001). *The Mind of War: John Boyd and American Security.* Washington, DC: Smithsonian.

Liker, J. (2004). *The Toyota way.* New York, NY: McGraw-Hill.

Musashi, M. (1982). Unattributed commentary to the second chapter. *The book of five rings.* (Nihon Services Group, Trans.) New York, NY: Bantam. (Original work published 1645).

Nissestad, O. A. (2007). *Leadership development: An empirical study of effectiveness of the leadership development program at The Royal Norwegian Naval Academy and its impact on preparing officers to execute leadership in today's conflicts and the conflicts in the years ahead*. (Doctoral dissertation). Norges Handelshøyskole (Norwegian School of Economics and Business Administration), Bergen (Norway).

Ohno, T. (1988). *Toyota Production System*. (Productivity Press, Trans.). Portland, OR: Productivity Press. (Original work published in 1978).

Osinga, F. P. B. (2005). *Science, strategy and war: The strategic theory of John Boyd*. (Doctoral dissertation). Delft (The Netherlands): Eburon Academic Publishers.

Osinga, F. P. B. (2006). *Science, strategy and war: The strategic theory of John Boyd*. London (UK): Routledge.

Peters, T. (2003). *Re-imagine! Business excellence in a disruptive age*. London (UK): Dorling Kindersley Publishing.

Richards, C. (2004). *Certain to win: The strategy of John Boyd, applied to business*. Philadephia, PA: Xlibris.

Royal Norwegian Naval Academy (2009). *Man the braces! The art of the moment for the benefit of the community*. Bergen (Norway): Royal Norwegian Naval Academy.

Sun Tzu (1988). *The art of war*. (T. Cleary Trans.) Boston, MA: Shambhala. (Date of original work unknown; generally thought to be c. 400 BCE).

Vandergriff, D. (2006). *Raising the bar*. Washington, DC: Center for Defense Information.

Ward, A., Liker, J. K., Cristiano, J. J., & Sobeck, D. K. II. (1995). The second Toyota paradox: How delaying decisions can make better cars faster. *Sloan Management Review*, 36 (3), 43-61.

Welch, J. & Welch S. (2005). *Winning*. New York, NY: HarperCollins.

Kanban System Archetypes

by

Karl Scotland, kscotlandl@rallydev.com

ABSTRACT

Many organisational challenges are a result of complex systemic issues, where cause and effect are not directly connected, but are separated by time and involve feedback loops and delays. Given that Kanban is a method for designing a product development system, and Systems Thinking includes the idea of system archetypes which describe common patterns of behaviour, we can use system archetypes to guide our design of Kanban systems and help us identify opportunities for improvement.

SYSTEMS THINKING

The original Agile methods were created by teams independently in response to the challenge of improving software development. Their documentation as a named process was a subsequent codification in order to help spread the learning and improvement wider throughout the industry. Either consciously or intuitively, these processes were applications of Systems Thinking, taking a holistic approach to solving the problem at hand. Taken in this context, we can learn from Agile methods by treating them as system archetypes rather than repeatable solutions, and design our own systems to create the same results.

SYSTEM STRUCTURE

Systems Thinking suggests that systems are made up of elements, which interact to meet a purpose. In other words, they are the product, rather than the sum of their parts.

- A system's purpose is what ultimately determines its behaviour. In fact, a system's purpose can be often deduced from its behaviour, which is observed over time rather than through individual events. A generic purpose for product development might be to deliver value through achieving flow and building capability.

- A system's elements are the things that it is made up of, and these can be either tangible or intangible. Tangible elements of a product development system could include the people, physical resources (e.g. hardware or furniture), and artefacts. Intangible elements could include the software itself (both product and tests), software tools (e.g. compilers and editors), skills, and morale.

- A system's interactions are the relationships that hold its elements together. They can typically be a flow of energy, material, or information. For product development systems, the most relevant interactions often take the form of information flows. This might be information about learning (e.g. success or failure), state changes (e.g. ready or done), or decisions (e.g. accepted or rejected).

SYSTEM FEEDBACK

A system can also be described in terms of stocks and flows. A stock is a recognisable and measurable part of the system, and the flows are what cause the stock to increase and decrease over time. Thus, the stock at any given time is the result of all the preceding flows in and out of the system. The stock acts as a buffer for the flows, which can create stability and allow for variability by decoupling the flows. However, it can also cause delays which may cause instability. In a product development system, if we think of the stock as the Work in Process (WIP), we can see that some WIP will create stability, and thus predictability, but too much will create undesirable delays.

Describing systems in terms of stocks and flows leads to the notion of feedback in systems. Feedback is created when changes in a stock affect the flows into or out of that same stock. There are two primary types of feedback: balancing and reinforcing.

Balancing Feedback

Balancing feedback will stabilise a system's behaviour. For example a thermostat is a balancing feedback system where the temperature is measured, the difference from the desired temperature measured, and a heating or cooling device adjustment made accordingly. This can be depicted as below, with the B identifying the loop as balancing. When the temperature is higher than the target, then the adjustment is to generate cold air. When the temperature is lower than the target, then the adjustment is to generate hot air.

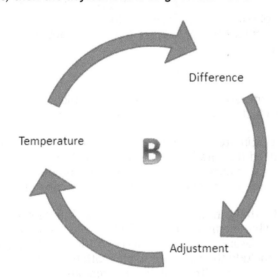

Reinforcing Feedback

Reinforcing feedback will amplify a system's behaviour. For example a bank account is a reinforcing feedback system where you have an account balance, onto which an interest rate is applied, and as a result you have interest paid to increase the balance (assuming your bank pays you interest). This can be depicted as below, with the R identifying the loop as balancing. As the cycle continues, more and more interest is paid, continually increasing your account balance. Conversely, when you have a negative account balance, your bank might apply a charge, which is deducted from your balance (much more likely). This cycle will continue as your account goes into increasing debt.

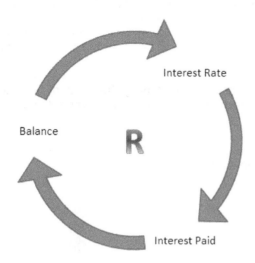

Delayed Feedback

What makes systems complex is that there are often delays in the feedback loops. Delays separate cause and effect over time which create complex non-linear behaviours and often leads to instability and oscillation. For example, as in the figure below, how many times have you been in the shower and tried to adjust the temperature, only to find the water suddenly gets too hot or cold? This is due to a delay between the action of adjusting the temperature and the temperature actually changing. As a result we tend to over-adjust and get burnt or chilled.

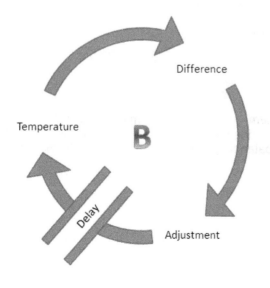

SYSTEM ARCHETYPES

Most systems are not as trivial as these examples, and consist of combinations of balancing and reinforcing feedback loops with different delays. However, a system's particular structure will result in its behaviour being constant over time, and systems with similar combinations result in similar behaviours. These patterns which cause similar and recognisable system behaviour are known as system archetypes.

Being able to recognise system archetypes helps to identify the cause of behaviours, and gives insight into how to break (or encourage) the archetype to our advantage. Let's take a look at an example.

Limits to Growth

The Limits to Success archetype can be depicted as below.

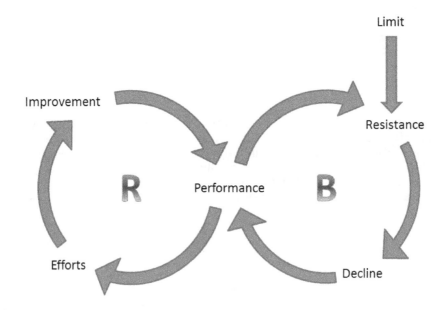

To improve performance of a system, more efforts are made, which do lead to the anticipated improvements, creating a reinforcing loop. However, after some time the performance reaches a limit and resistance creates a balancing loop, leading to the performance leveling off, declining, or even crashing.

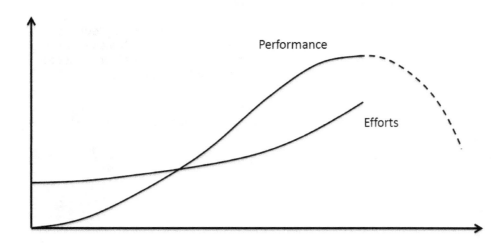

Recognising this archetype leads to the understanding that when the system resists, or pushes back on attempts at improvement, rather than continuing to push the reinforcing loop and increase efforts or do the same thing better, we should instead look to remove the limits by adjusting the system design to delaying the balancing loop. In other words, deal with the limits before the system does. Allowing the system to define the limits will result in a worse outcome.

A Kanban system can help to cope with Limits to Success in a couple of ways.

- Firstly, setting explicit Work in Process limits is a way of directly limiting the system before the system does so itself, avoiding the decline or crash in performance.

- Secondly, gaining transparency of the work and the workflow is a beginning to learning what the cause of the limiting factor is. Visualizing any bottlenecks or impediments gives a good indication of where to start looking to make changes in the system design to remove its limits.

CONCLUSION

These simple Systems Thinking concepts give us a clue to how we can help meet the challenges that come with improving our product development practices, without resorting to codifying methods. Having clarity of purpose, and the way a system's elements interact to achieve that purpose, can give us insight into intervention points for continuously improving.

System archetypes give us a further perspective with which to view our product development processes, and suggests a role Kanban plays. If Agile processes are examples of system archetypes, then Kanban provides an approach to creating further examples of those system archetypes. Workflow can be thought of as part of the system structure. Visualization can highlight key elements and interactions. Limiting WIP can manage the stock. Cadence can help coordination of elements and interactions. Learning can focus on improving the system. Further, where processes are exhibiting less desirable archetypes, then Kanban provides an approach to recognise and visualize them, and leverage points to eventually break them.

Donella H. Meadows eloquently wrote that "The future can't be predicted, but it can be envisioned and brought lovingly into being" and "We can't control systems or figure them out. But we can dance with them!" Kanban provides a means to dance with our product development systems while we lovingly envision them and bring them into being.

REFERENCE
Meadows, D.H. (2008). Thinking in Systems: A Primer. White River Junction, VT: Chelsea Green Publishing.

Lean Software Development Comes of Age

by

Alan Shalloway, alshall@netobjectives.com

ABSTRACT

While lean may have sprung from Toyota, there is a large enough body of knowledge about how and why lean works, as well as how to transition an organization to manifest it so that it can stand on its own. This paper briefly discusses the history of Lean Software Development and argues that, however it came in to existence, it is more effective to think of it on its own terms. This paper discusses why Lean Software Development can (and should) be thought of as a combination of science, management, and learning. This creates the foundation for future development and understanding.

LEAN SOFTWARE DEVELOPMENT COMES OF AGE

Actually, it came of age years ago, but nobody noticed until recently. What do I mean "comes of age"? I mean it can stand on its own. To many, Lean Software Development comes from the translation of the lean principles of manufacturing into the world of software by Mary and Tom Poppendieck in 2003[1]. Actually, the notions of lean software development had been written about by Bob Charette in the 90s, and also done well before that[2]. Don Reinertsen was writing about the equivalent of Lean product development in 1997 with his Managing the Design Factory, only he didn't call it Lean.

Where Did Lean Software Development Come From?

Lean software can be thought of in many different ways, mostly because Lean can be thought of in many different ways. What exactly is *Lean*? Well, that's the root of the question. Womack and Jones, two of the principal authors of the book that originally defined Lean, provided a set of five principles in their follow up book *Lean Thinking*: value, value stream, flow, pull, and perfection.

Of course, one can go back to the source, Taiichi Ohno, the man credited with creating the Toyota Production System. Mr. Ohno describes what they do at Toyota (they don't call it "Lean") as based on two principles: "Just-in-time" and "autonomation" (automation with a human touch). Of course, he was not elaborating on the foundation that Toyota had that most of us do not: Deming[3]. Deming's system of profound knowledge includes:

---

1   Lean Software Development: An Agile Toolkit.
2   James Sutton, co-author of Lean Software Strategies: Proven Techniques for Managers and Developers, related how he started doing lean in software in the late 80s.
3   Edwards Deming is the man pretty much credited with enabling the Japanese to turn around their manufacturing methods, which in the late 1940s were in an abysmal state, to where just 30-40 years later they were considered the best in the world.

1. An appreciation for a system.
2. Knowledge about variation.
3. Theory of knowledge.
4. Knowledge of psychology.

So one could say Ohno's principles were improving the system by having management teach people how to improve their methods of working while achieving just-in-time and improving quality by detecting errors immediately. But it is more than this, because one of the more salient characteristics of Toyota is its continuous method of learning and improvement that is driven by employees and shepherded by management.

All of this, of course, is complicated by the fact that the Toyota Production System (TPS) is about manufacturing and Lean is also about product development — the Toyota Product Development System (TPDS). The Poppendiecks generally translated the TPS into software in their first book, moving more into the area of product development in their second book, *Lean Software Development: From Concept to Cash.*

Don Reinertsen discusses Lean from a series of insights on how to quickly create products that are economically viable (*Managing the Design Factory* and *The Principles of Product Development Flow: 2nd Generation Lean Product Development*). He has come to Lean completely independently from Toyota, taking advantage of his background as a Navy helmsman and successful business consultant. His fundamental belief is you need great systems with great people attending to development products quickly, since time is the most important variable in product development. While Reinertsen's work was about product development, not software development, it is generally recognized now that software development *is* a kind of product development. So, if one understands Lean *product* development, one will have great insights into Lean *software* development[4].

No wonder it's all confusing when getting an answer as to what Lean Software Development is. Who are you building from (Ohno, Womack & Jones, Reinertsen) and do you use manufacturing or product development as the base?

Lean Software Development Re-Defined

I'll admit that I'm not that interested in historical accuracy. I'm more interested in how one can think of Lean in a way that would be useful. I would suggest that the start of this is not to think of Lean as something that emanated from someone or something else. Doing so will have us stuck on ideas that may have become outdated. We must avoid cargo cultism[5], an all-too-common characteristic of the software community. Instead, I suggest we look at Lean Software Development as a body of knowledge in its own right. This also has the advantage of not being dependent

---

4   Managing the Design Factory continues to be my most recommended book to date. (Never mind that it was written 14 years ago; it was 20 years ahead of its time.)
5   Cargo cult refers to the mistaken beliefs of pre-industrialized cultures that came into contact with industrialized societies. Cargo cult activity in the Pacific region increased significantly during and immediately after World War II, when the residents of these regions observed the Japanese and American combatants bringing in large amounts of material. When the war ended, the military bases closed and the flow of goods and materials ceased. In an attempt to attract further deliveries of goods, followers of the cults engaged in ritualistic practices such as building crude imitation landing strips, aircraft, and radio equipment, and mimicking the behavior that they had observed of the military personnel operating them. Many software methods have embraced a cultism of belief in how they work that is not based in reality, but rather on past instances of success with no real understanding as to why it works or fails.

on any of the methods of a particular practitioner[6].

My own view of Lean is that it is comprised of three different components, all of which are interrelated. These are: Lean Science, Lean Management, and Lean Learning.

LEAN SCIENCE

By Lean science I mean those laws of reality that affect software development. Sometimes these are called principles. But principles take one of two forms:

1. They can be rules that describe how the universe works (e.g., the law of gravity).

2. They can be guidance for how to behave (e.g., tell the truth).

In Lean science, I am referring to laws, not guidance — although clearly, we'll figure out guidance based on the laws. The valuing of Lean science follows from Deming's view of looking at the system for errors, not at the people. In our book, *Lean-Agile Software Development: Achieving Enterprise Agility*, we present the following laws of software development:

- Shortening cycle time will reduce waste and increase quality.

- You tend to get waste and lower quality when you increase the time between:
    - When you need information and when you get it.
    - When you make an error until you discover the error.

- Making decisions too early increases the risk of waste.

- Excess Work In Progress (WIP) increases both risk and waste.

- Impediments to flow cause waste.

- Increasing the number of concurrent projects with a given amount of resources working them increases the length of the projects.

- Large batches cause waste.

- Switching from one task to another such that thrashing occurs causes waste.

- Having people work on more than one project at a time decreases their efficiency.

- Not paying attention to risk may cause waste.

- Delivering value quickly increases ROI.

There are, of course, others. But these illustrate that there *are* laws of software development. Practitioners need to know them.

LEAN MANAGEMENT

Management of software seems to provide one with two choices: micro-manage, or having

---

6   While I consider myself "pre-cognitive impaired," I did give a presentation at the Miami Lean/Kanban talk in 2009 (prior to Toyota's brake meltdown) called "Redefining Lean," where I discussed how Lean could be considered a body of knowledge in its own right, separate from Toyota. My intent then was to mitigate any risk of Toyota falling away from its own principles — which they subsequently did, in fact, do.

the inmates run the asylum (also referred to as "herding cats"). The problem is that most developers consider themselves craftsman or artists, while many managers don't really understand the intricacies of software development. This leaves one in the predicament of either over-managing or over-trusting. Lean provides a better way. If Lean science truly exists, it opens up a new paradigm for management.

Many managers got where they are because they are good problem solvers. It's hard for them to sit by when a problem comes up. They want to jump in and solve it. This, however, leads to micro-management and creates lost opportunities for the manager's charges.

Lean suggests using visual controls to explicitly represent the work taking place. A visual control is a visual and explicit representation of the work taking place. It should represent both what the agreed methods of working are as well as how well the team is following them. The visual control is not a grading measure. Rather, it's a reflection of the work taking place. It provides visibility so that the team members can ensure they are following the process they as a team have decided is best. This process can and should change on a regular basis as the team learns better ways of working.

With visual controls in place, managers can see how their teams are doing. They don't have to resort to micro-management, but rather can coach the teams to improve as well as question the teams if they stop following what they themselves say is the best way to do things.

LEAN LEARNING

The true, key distinguishing piece of Lean is Lean learning. This is what truly distinguishes Lean companies from those that are not. It is not just the science they use, but rather how they have their people learn. Lean management combined with Lean science creates the opportunity for what I call Lean learning. It is actually continuous learning based on learning how our actions affect our work.

It is best described in Michael Rother's brilliant book *Toyota Kata*. Rother describes what he calls the "improvement and coaching kata." The improvement kata is how to both learn and teach. That is, one can use it by oneself, but Rother explains how Toyota managers use it to teach their people how to solve problems. The coaching kata is how one teaches managers how to do the improvement kata.

The improvement kata consists in asking five questions which help you look at how your process works instead of just the results you are achieving. These questions are:

> "Excellence is not an act, but a habit."
>
> - Aristotle

1. What is your target condition (that is, what do you want to achieve)?

2. What is your actual condition (that is, what *have* you achieved)?

3. What obstacles are now preventing you from reaching your target condition (and which

one are you addressing now)?

4. What is your next step?

5. When can we go and see what we have learned from taking that step?

The improvement kata allows for continuous cycles of small learnings. It is essentially one way to manifest Deming's famed PDSA cycle (Plan Do Study Act).

Putting it Together

Lean is not quite the sum of its parts, however. It is more. The biggest difference between Lean and agile methods is the perspective of how to apply them. Lean comes from the entire system perspective — the Poppendiecks' "optimize the whole." In other words, Lean suggests looking at the whole value stream when improving an organization, not merely try to repeat local successes on a larger scale[7].

To create a Lean-enterprise one must manage drive from the business needs, manage the portfolio of potential products/projects to be worked on, and feed a team that will use lean methods. We need to focus on the smallest pieces of functionality that are worth the transaction cost to deliver. Some people call these minimal marketable features[8].

> "Sustained success is largely a matter of focusing regularly on the right things and making a lot of uncelebrated little improvements every day."
>
> - Theodore Levitt, Harvard Business School

Lean science, management, and learning can manifest themselves in the entire organization. Lean science's theory of flow tells us that by focusing on removing delays between the work steps we have (or by eliminating the handoffs by not having discrete steps), we can reduce the time from when we start working on something until it can be consumed by the customer (external for a product company, internal for an IT organization). By reducing this time we should expect both an increase in quality as well as a decrease in cost[9].

Let's look at how the Virtual Kanban System for Software Development (or Kanban for short) is a manifestation of Lean science, Lean management, and Lean learning in action. Kanban is a method of managing how many things you have in progress at one time. The idea of a Kanban card to limit work is best related by a story David Anderson tells in his seminal work "Kanban: Successful Evolutionary Change for Your Technology Business," which I'll retell here from my own personal experience. A few years ago I visited Tokyo and stayed near the Imperial Gardens. When my wife and I entered the gardens we were each given a white card that simply said "please return to attendant upon leaving." No money exchanged hands; in fact, only a smile and nod were exchanged. Why did they give us these cards? Essentially, it is a low cost, imprecise way of limiting the number of people in the gardens. While it is possible that people would enter from one

---

7   In fact, this attempt at scaling often leads to successful pilots that take the organization further away from agility. See my blog *How Successful Pilots Often Actually Hurt an Organization*.

8   This term was first introduced by Deene and Cleeland-Huang in *Software By Numbers*.

9   See a 10 minute video "How Delays Cause Waste" at http://www.youtube.com/netobjectives for a better understanding of this.

side and leave from another (there are about half a dozen entrances), it is more likely that the general entry/exit flow will be balanced. When the attendants run out of cards, people outside have to wait to get in.

Kanban cards in the software world work pretty much the same way. WIP limits are one way to achieve a simple method of work control. Kanban combines Lean science, Lean management, and Lean learning, which is, in my mind, why it is becoming the clear choice for managing development organizations. Let's look at how it does this.

Lean Science. Kanban is best known for limiting the amount of WIP so as to not exceed the capacity of the team. This is because exceeding that capacity leads to delays, which leads to extra work and lower quality. Kanban uses both the principles of Lean flow as well as the theory of constraints in managing WIP so as to alleviate any constraints in the system.

Lean Management. Kanban uses visual controls to manage the work of the team. A Kanban board is a reflection of the work of the team. However, Kanban insists that the workflow be explicitly defined. This explicitness has several advantages including better communication and making the team's understanding explicit. However, it also enables both Lean management and Lean learning as we will shortly discuss. This explicitness is one of the significant differences between Kanban and Scrum and significantly adds to the potential of positive management involvement. By having explicit policies, management can see how the team is working. This visibility is not an invitation to meddle, but it does provide two other opportunities. The first is that management can see how what they do affects the team. When management doesn't understand the workings of a team, it is all too easy for them to ask for "just one more thing." A little extra effort is all it takes[10].

Kanban's explicit Kanban board will enable management to see how any extra demands will affect the team. This same visibility is often useful for management (either a real manager or a team leader) to assist with doing an improvement kata. It was actually these two characteristics of Kanban — management can see the effect they have on the team and the team can continuously learn in small steps due to explicit policies — that got me interested in Kanban as the primary method for running development organizations. Seeing where you are, improving it on a continual basis, and including management have been things I had only rarely seen demonstrated in a sustained manner by Scrum teams.

When one adds to the fact that Kanban is one of the few (only?) agile methods that enables an organization to always start, it seems like a clear winner. This aspect was particularly important to me as a consultant. Prior to learning Kanban, I had a handful of what I considered failures where I could not convince companies to make the leap to agile methods with Scrum. Some of these were due to the fact that the jump was beyond their comfort level. Some of these were due to some people having specialized skills where they could not be placed on one team, but had to be shared across teams — something Scrum gives little insights on. The bottom line was, the challenges I could not solve without Kanban could be readily solved with it.

It was also apparent that even where cross-functional teams could be created, and even when you wanted to do iterations, all of the practices of Kanban (visibility, explicit policies, man-

---

10   Anyone who has been on a development team knows this is not true, but this is the mindset of many managers.

aging WIP, continual learning, use of flow) improved other agile methods. We have therefore incorporated them into our Scrum practices as well. The only question there is: Do you call it Scrum with Lean or Kanban with iterations? We prefer to call it the latter because Kanban with iterations is essentially the same as Kanban with cadence. Scrum with Kanban's mindset is considerably different than the black-box process still espoused by many in the Scrum community.

CONCLUSION

While to most, Lean originated with Toyota, thinking of Lean Software Development as an extension of manufacturing practices is not as effective as looking at Lean as a body of knowledge in its own right. Lean software includes rules that organizations will find valuable. This opens up the possibility for management to provide coaching/education in these rules. It further enables management to see the effects they have on the teams they work with. This enables them to avoid adverse meddling, while providing guidance and structure that can improve the teams. Continuous learning is a result. Perhaps the biggest difference, however, is the mindset that lean provides — one of looking at the entire picture and not merely trying to scale a successful team pilot project and hope that will solve the organization's problems. Lean has truly come of age in two ways. First, it can stand on its own regardless of where you feel it originated. Second, it demonstrates that it is an essential paradigm for enterprise agility.

REFERENCES

Anderson, David (2010) *Kanban: Successful Evolutionary Change for Your Technology Business.* Seattle, WA: Free Hole Press.

Middleton, Peter & Sutton, James. (2005) *Lean Software Strategies: Proven Techniques for Managers and Developers.* New York, NY: Productivity Press.

Poppendieck, Mary & Poppendieck, Tom. (2003) *Lean Software Development: An Agile Toolkit.* Boston, MA: Addison Wesley.

Reinertsen, Donald. (1997) *Managing the Design Factory.* New York, NY: Free Press.

Shalloway, Alan. (2010) *How Successful Pilots Often Actually Hurt an Organization.* http://www.netobjectives.com/blogs/how-successful-pilots-can-hurt-the-organization.

A large Kanban implementation:

What happened when the principle of viral spread suffered from the success

by

Jasper Sonnevelt, mail@jaspersonnevelt.nl

ABSTRACT

In a company that is generally slow moving and risk averse (a Benelux insurance company), after a successful pilot with multiple teams the decision is made to make Kanban the preferred method of operating in software development and maintenance teams. This decision has a big impact as it violates the principle of viral spread. This article explains what this has done to teams, productivity, transparency, employees, and costs. Pros, cons, and expected and unexpected successes will be discussed, as well as best practices and things we tried that did not have the desired effect.

INTRODUCTION

In August of 2009 the company started a pilot to see if Kanban would be a viable method to use in software development teams for incidents and small software changes (up to 400 hours). The goal was to get a better grip on the software development process, lower costs, and increase quality, transparency, team involvement, and engagement.

When this pilot proved a success the decision was made to make this the preferred method of operation for software development in maintenance and operations teams. In February 2010, 12 teams started with Kanban for incident management and in April another 12 started to implement the changes.

In this article I will tell you about the status now (roughly seven months after the second batch of teams started) some of the challenges faced and tackled, and also the challenges still facing the teams and the organizations, along with some general observations about the teams.

STATUS

When a new environment was created for the people to work in Kanban teams there was a change in the organization's structure as well. In this new structure there are three types of teams. The first, which was in the old structure as well, is the project team. Most of these are using Scrum and usually work on projects larger than 1,000 hours. The second type of team has as its main objective to make sure continuity of applications is warranted. The last team does small changes and maintenance on applications. All three types of teams work for one business line and use Kanban. This is so that the business line always has one contact in each team instead of a multitude as in the old environment.

This change in how the ICT organization was structured had a (mostly mental) big impact on the team members. In the situation prior to the decision to restructure the IT organization, resource teams would allocate resources for small maintenance and development and allocate the rest of the team members to larger (bigger than 1,000 hours) projects. These teams were technology (for instance J2EE or dotNet) oriented instead of Business Line oriented. Instead of working in a team of developers that work on the same platform, people are now expected to work in multidisciplinary teams. They're not just responsible for their own technology but instead they're part of a team that as a whole is responsible for the software they develop. This means having business representatives sitting across from you and telling you what they need and what has priority. People to whom you can ask questions when you have them. Being able to see every incident that occurs in your business line. Sounds great, right? Yes. Definitely. However, the change from the old to the new world was very sudden, and for some people who had been working in the same department on the same technology for almost 40 years it might have been too sudden.

On the other side were people who had already seen the success of the pilot, or had even been in it, and had seen what it was like to work in a Kanban team. For instance, one development team had achieved a 60% drop in lead-times. Another example: the teams responsible for the continuity had, without having a full end-to-end collaboration and some teams that aren't working with Kanban (just a board, a multidisciplinary team, and stand-ups) reduced the size of their total backlog by 10% and are 15% under budget. These teams, without proper resources and working according to prescribed methods were able to achieve results.

VIOLATION OF A KEY PRINCIPLE AND WHAT THIS DOES TO TEAMS

When the organization was restructured, and Kanban was to be used as the standard way of working in most of the software development and maintenance teams, one of the key principles of Kanban was violated: viral spread.

When the pilot ended there were in total seven teams working with Kanban, some of them as a part of the pilot and others as a result of viral spread. Responses were positive, and even though not everybody knew the ins and outs of Kanban, most of teams were able to achieve the goals they set themselves at the start. A thing all these teams had in common was that they all chose to use Kanban and knew why.

Team morale

After the change in February some teams were no longer clear on why Kanban was chosen. Some people didn't even want to be in a team. "I just want to work on my platform (A) and I honestly do not care about platform B".

It is important to know that some of these people had been working on their platform for a long time. They were set in their ways and good at what they did.

This, and the fact that a rapid expansion brings a number of new challenges to the table, caused the team morale to go down a bit in the majority of the teams. Being consistent and not giving up or allowing the teams to go back to their old way of working whilst at the same time explaining the "why" and "why now" has shown a slight increase in team morale after a few months.

CHALLENGES

A challenge for the teams at this point is to keep improving. It is clearly visible that after a couple of months the rush of having a new way of working has worn off. Now it is imperative to keep stimulating the continuous improvement of this way of working, while trying not to be put down by the fact that the company is redesigning its whole structure, and to focus on the process.

Other challenges are the economic crisis, changing the mindset of the team members, and achieving real end-to-end collaboration. At this point most of the teams still don't have people from infrastructure in their team, which is a problem when you want to deploy the software.

CHALLENGES STILL FACING US

(Out) sourcing

How to use Kanban when your ICT strategy is (out) sourcing? Due to cost reductions, out-sourcing is becoming more and more an option when the software development strategy is "reuse before buy before make". But how do you (want to) work with a third party if you have Kanban teams in your own organization? This is a question that is becoming increasingly more urgent in the organization. If you were to include third party companies in your Kanban process, are the teams you have working mature enough to do so?

At this moment the challenges the teams face with end-to-end collaboration are made more explicit with the increasing amount of teams with both onshore and offshore team members. Team members realize this and respond in different ways. More mature teams respond by looking for possibilities. These are not necessarily the teams with the most senior (in a Kanban way of working) team members. The teams review their own process and adapt accordingly. A thing that distinguishes these teams from teams that have more problems adapting to this change is that they don't question the way of working. They still want to have stand-ups, retrospectives, and a board for visual management. Most of the teams have not yet solved all the problems. Some teams like to have stand-ups where one person has been brought up to speed with the activities of the offshore team members; others have experimented with video screens. At this point there is not yet a way of working that "works best".

Rapid expansion

More and more teams still want to (or have to) use Kanban. The problem is that there are not enough people in the organization to adequately train and coach these teams. There have been multiple occasions where the question, "And what tips for coaching can you give me?" has been asked in a Kanban introduction presentation. The result of this absence of sufficiently trained coaches and facilitators is that team successes are becoming closer related to the skills of the facilitator and / or coach than to the team itself.

End-to-end collaboration

A challenge that was facing us when we started with the first 12 teams was the end-to-end collaboration in the software development chain. This was not completely realized when the pilot ended and was one of the things that would be arranged when the new teams started. This partially has happened. When the 12 teams started, they were a little different than the teams in the pilot. In the pilot the teams were technology oriented. The first team had only Java developers and testers. No infrastructure (which was needed for deployments to test and production environments) and no business representation.

The new teams, though, were supposed to start with business representation from the beginning. The customer would be right next to us. For some teams this was actually realized, for others not. The most heard excuse was that there was not enough work to put people dedicated in the teams. Looking back from a neutral perspective, the reason probably (also) was that we did not communicate well enough why it was so important to have the customer represented in our teams.

We were able to make the difference visible by starting to measure not just work time and availability of software, but also measuring customer satisfaction. Comparing this data there were some interesting conclusions.

- Teams that had business representation in their teams could have a lower availability whilst still having a higher customer satisfaction.

- The same teams were able to decrease the size of the (incident) backlog even at times when the inflow increased.

OBSERVATIONS

Digital vs. physical boards and team engagement

Along with the introduction of the new teams a new way of working for the organization was also introduced. In this new form people can sit wherever they want instead of having their own desk. To make this possible everybody was issued a laptop and a mobile phone. This also stimulated the possibilities of working at home and on other locations. Not long after this was started the questions began to arise about how to do Kanban with a physical board, and not long after that digital boards were introduced. This brought along a whole new set of challenges. For instance, suddenly people didn't think a stand-up was that important anymore.

As with most things that stand in the way of teams being successful, more mature teams responded in a more mature way than the teams that weren't that far along.

However, it is worth noting that team engagement does tend to suffer when team members are not doing stand-ups on a regular basis (daily or a minimum of three times a week). Other ways of getting the team more engaged have to be explored. One way to increase engagement is by increasing the responsibilities of individual team members for the end product.

Facilitator skills

As mentioned in the "Challenges" section the results of teams seem to be, because of the absence of enough sufficiently trained coaches and facilitators, more dependent on the skills of the facilitator than on the team itself. This stands in the way of the teams reaching a state of independence. A sign of this is that they don't do stand-ups when the facilitator is not present. If they do it, it usually is longer than 15 minutes or is done in a very different way.

Another thing that jumped to attention when there turned out to be too few sufficiently experienced facilitators and coaches is that the teams that did respond very well to the rapid expansion of the amount of Kanban teams also adapted to this change very well. They managed to keep the team running and the work flowing with the key principles in mind. They might change things, but they remembered to communicate it to their environment and stakeholders. The team that managed to do this best has even improved the communication within the team itself because the team members tried to explain to everybody around them what they were doing.

CONCLUSIONS

Looking back on the situation we started from, the improvements we made, and the progress the teams made there are a few conclusions to be drawn.

First and foremost, don't assume that because a pilot has proven successful and because other teams quickly adapted to the new way of working that this will also happen when the new way of working gets promoted to the standard way of working. A shift is made from people who want to work like this to people who have to work like this. It's no longer a "sexy" way of working. It's standard. You're no longer the early adopter. Going from pilot and viral spread to standard way of working means that you will have to think about different things other than proving it works. Suddenly facilitating, coaching, and training become much more important than they already were. So before you promote a successful pilot to the standard method of working in a large organization, plan ahead. Realize that there will be changes and different aspects to this implementation than to the pilot.

Secondly, when there is not enough knowledge and experience available to keep the same facilitator:team and coach:facilitator ratio, team members get the chance to make their mark on the team. Of course this has consequences for the way teams adopt the Kanban philosophy and principles, but given the circumstances this has worked out for some of the teams.

Leading Your Business Customer:

A Case Study of A3 Thinking and why it Works

by

Dean C. Stevens, Dean.Stevens@Synaptus.com

ABSTRACT

Two top success factors for successful IT projects are user involvement and executive support. A3 thinking helps to achieve both of these. The A3 process is simply a means to facilitate A3 thinking. This paper is not necessarily a how-to on the A3 process. Instead I focus on the thinking behind the process by walking through a case study and highlighting the thinking elements required to support learning, change, and results.

INTRODUCTION

The Director of Marketing told the project team, "I want an online presence like Amazon," and he had already selected the new web application he intended to use. This is the beginning of an actual case that was mentioned in an HBR article a couple of years ago, "The Next Revolution in Productivity." The article explained how we decided to focus on improving the business capability *Post Accessory Catalog Electronically* as a high priority. This is the rest of the story of how we used A3 thinking to give the director what he actually needed.

Why A3 Thinking?

Technology leaders supporting business operations must deliver technology solutions that make a difference to the business. The problem is that business users do not always really know what they want and business executives do not always really know what they are buying. All too often, the technology group is asked to build solutions without having a clear enough understanding of the problem, solution, or options.

This problem is highlighted by the Standish Group's "Chaos Summary Report 2009" that concludes the top two success factors for IT projects continue to be User Involvement and Executive Support. Since these factors are critical to the technology group's success, they had better have a way to engage users and gain executive support. The A3 approach, done well, accomplishes this.

What is an A3? Think of it simply as an illustrated storyline telling how a problem was solved, created collaboratively with stakeholders perhaps on a whiteboard, and presented briefly. But it is more than another requirements document in what it accomplishes. John Shook describes its potential in the title of his book, "Managing to Learn: Using the A3 management process to solve problems, gain agreement, mentor and lead." It can certainly be used to engage business users and gain executive support.

The purpose of this paper is to illustrate seven specific thinking elements to prompt the critical thinking necessary to address complex problems in a business.

A3 Storyline

The A3 Storyline when done well, that is when it is used to achieve A3 thinking elements, implements an improvement model, a set of principles, to deliver business results. In this case study, we are following Lean Principles, although A3 thinking can be applied based on other models as well. The Lean Principles are Specify Value, Map the Value Stream, Create Flow, Establish Pull, and Continuous Improvement. A3 thinking is how you fill the gap between these Lean Principles and "What do we do now?"

First, consider these three basic A3 Thinking Elements.

Thinking Element: Logical Thinking Process

The A3 Storyline is how Toyota implements PDCA: Plan, Do, Check/Study, Adjust. It is a solid, proven approach to project planning, allowing for an appropriate degree and depth of thinking based on the context and scope of the situation. The basic requirement is to do enough of each part to tell a meaningful story. Of course the challenge is to know what "enough" is. Only experience and mentoring can address that challenge. The A3 management process is basically a problem solving approach. Consider it a lightweight alternative to ad hoc problem solving, providing a better chance of project success.

Thinking Element: Objectivity

Use the A3 thinking to provide an objective focus. Look for facts. Look for cause and effect relationships. Experiment if you are not sure. Check that solutions address the problem. A team's chance of solving a problem is much better if the solution is rooted in reality.

Thinking Element: Results and Process

A3 thinking is as much about professional development as it is about achieving results. A small investment in discipline around the A3 process will deliver both better results and team learning.

A3 Process Step 1: Grasp the Situation

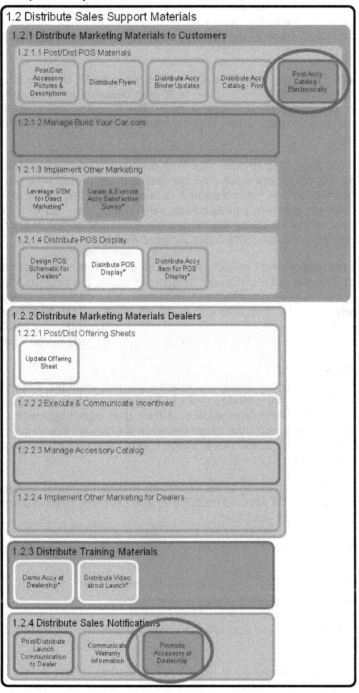

First the team investigated the background and current condition of the problem space. A Value Network Map (VNM) revealed that the firm's ability to *Distribute Sales Support Materials* was a key strategic focus. A deep dive into this area further revealed that improving the firm's ability to *Post Accessory Catalog* and *Promote Accessories at Dealership* were the major problems in this area.

The VNM is heat-mapped through structured interviews using colors to visualize the value and performance of each business activity. Reading the heat-map becomes intuitive quickly with a little explanation. The border color represents business value. The fill color indicates performance gap. A red color indicates high value or gap. Green is low; yellow is moderate. So, we focus on very red activities or hot spots.

The heat-map reveals that *Post Accessory Catalog* was determined to have very high business value (red border) and performed very poorly for end users (red fill). And without a good e-catalog, *Promoting Accessories at the Dealership* was extremely problematic (also red border, red fill). Interestingly, addressing the e-catalog would provide a foundation for improving many other activities to *Distribute Sales Support Materials.*

Our opportunity statement became clear while investigating this problem. We drafted a statement to Specify Value, the first principle of the Lean approach. Our customers and end users, auto dealers and buyers respectively, valued a "consolidated catalog including DIO/LIO accessories with accurate and complete information to facilitate the sales process." It was in the presentation of these initial findings that the Director of Marketing made his proclamation.

Thinking Element: Systems Viewpoint
W. Edwards Deming writes about the importance of a systems viewpoint. Deming holds his First Principle of the System of Profound Knowledge (SoPK) to be *Appreciation for a System*. He explains that "a system is a network of interdependent activities that work together to try to accomplish the aim of the system." This is what the Value Network Map shows visually. Deming goes on to write, "A system must be managed. It will not manage itself." The rest of the process guides us to responsibly managing the system.

Peter Senge also holds systems thinking to be important in organizational management in his seminal book *The Fifth Discipline: The Art and Practice of the Learning Organization*. Systems thinking is the fifth and final discipline he discusses.

To apply a systems viewpoint pragmatically, we must develop an understanding of:

- The purpose of the course of action.

- How the course of action furthers the organization's goals.

- How it fits into the larger picture and affects other parts of the organization (Sobek and Smalley 2008).

Our effort to *Grasp the Situation* should at least begin to address these points. In our case, we have articulated our opportunity statement to understand our purpose or aim. We have a Value Network Map that generally models the system and visualizes how stakeholders view the value and performance of each activity. We have started to learn. It is important to note that what we reported earlier is the end result of investigation, interactions, and interviews. The team is telling a story of what we learned and validated together. **A3 Process Step 2: Analysis**

We wanted to validate that data errors were indeed a systematic problem and not a few special instances. A couple of team members performed a quick data analysis and found that 16% of recent items had errors. Older items were much worse. We had a problem. We also had a benchmark to check whether our solution helped.

The team gathered at a whiteboard with post-it notes. We quickly mapped out the process to *Post Accessory Catalog*. Then we changed it and moved post-its and talked about it until we agreed we had it right — or at least close. Next, we walked the process, talking to the people actually doing the work. We showed them the board and kept rearranging until, finally, we all agreed. Then we marked the problems in red. This did not really take very long, but we learned how things currently worked together and where the real problems were.

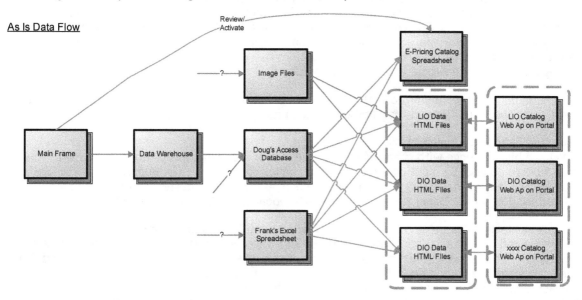

Next, using a whiteboard and post-it notes again, we thought about the root causes using a fishbone diagram and then discussing the 5 Whys. Where were the interruptions to information flow? Why? What was the impact that kept us from achieving value, especially "accurate and complete information?" Below is what we found. We shared our whiteboard work with as many stakeholders as we could before recording it on the A3 report.

IDENTIFY WASTE: Lines in red indicate waste.
1. Manual work that takes more time than necessary and results in errors and missing information.
2. HTML files difficult to manage automatically. Review of information problematic.
3. Multiple catalogs cause dealer associates to toggle between LIO and DIO to gather information for customers . Customer desires one place to find all accessories for a model.

Thinking Element: Synthesis, Distillation, and Visualization

An important aspect of the A3 thinking is that we report our findings briefly. Traditionally, the A3 report is produced on a single A3 (11x17) sheet of paper. Consider it an executive brief. Figuring out what not to say and how to communicate is challenging. Synthesize all you have learned. Distill learnings to key points. Visualize with pictures, graphs, and numbers. You cannot accomplish this until you and your team have clarity of thinking. You will be much more persuasive. Your audience will appreciate the brevity and are more likely to actually pay attention. Don't worry; you get to tell the story. Conversations carry the detail and tacit knowledge. You are taking responsibility for more effective communication.

In our case, we managed with very few words because the organization participated in developing the Value Network Map and understood it.

Thinking Element: Alignment

A big challenge with change is that one group or individual has to do more while another may have to do less. By focusing on flow and obstacles to flow of value, people can better understand why change is necessary. They may not like it, but they will better understand. Sharing the A3 findings, either the paper report or on the whiteboard, is important to gain alignment.

Achieving alignment requires 3D communication. Communicate back and forth in time so people can understand your thinking process and where you anticipate going. Communicate horizontally across the organization by sharing with your team members and others affected. Then they communicate up and down the hierarchy to their direct reports and managers who then talk to each other. An important note is to share as much as possible prior to meetings. The last thing you want to do is present an unpopular change unvetted in a meeting and have the ideas questioned or rejected. Better to have your ideas rejected or questioned more privately. If this sounds like a lot of work, this consensus building, it can be in some organizations. You cannot gain buy-in from everyone for every detail. At some point you may have to get a small group of stakeholders together to hash out differences. Do what makes sense in your situation and organization with a bias for over-communicating.

In our case, the team was excited to be part of solving a persistent problem to an important part of the business. Alignment is much more likely when team members and business users are advocates.

Again, what we reported is the end result of investigation, interactions, and interviews. We are adding to the story of what we have learned and validated together.

A3 Process Step 3: Solutions

The Director of Marketing now, somewhat reluctantly, accepted that the problem was with product information management and a new web application would not solve that. The team members had been thinking about solutions even before they really understood the problem. Now that they had earned that understanding, it was time consider options. Because we had intentionally included a broad set of stakeholders including business users, a few dealers, and IT, we were able to generate and begin to consider several options quickly that addressed our primary root causes. One option was to hire and train more people. At the other end of the spectrum was to fully automate the process. I actually suggested both of these extremes to open the session and help make any suggestion safe. A marketing manager had been investigating a canned product information management system. Doug really liked his Access database and wasn't sure anything else could perform as well. Kevin just wanted help.

Once the solutions brainstorming session was done, we left to reflect on our work and consider the options (although I suspect most went to catch up on emails and phone calls since their real job was to run the business). We reconvened after a few days to evaluate the proposed solution sets. The team reviewed each solution set, considering pros and cons, asking clarifying questions, and considering the impact of addressing root causes. The team sponsor participated and reserved his opinions and questions until everyone else had contributed.

Once the team was satisfied with its understanding of each solution set, we met again to make our recommendations. In this workshop, the team members made strong arguments as others provided different views. We agreed to propose a couple of solution sets for the project sponsor's consideration. Here is what we settled on.

ELIMINATE WASTE:

1. Consolidate accessory information into one database. This eliminates to need to manually update a variety of HTML files.
2. Eliminate HTML interface and pull information directly from the consolidated database.

FLOW WHERE YOU CAN, PULL WHERE YOU MUST

Proposed Data Flow

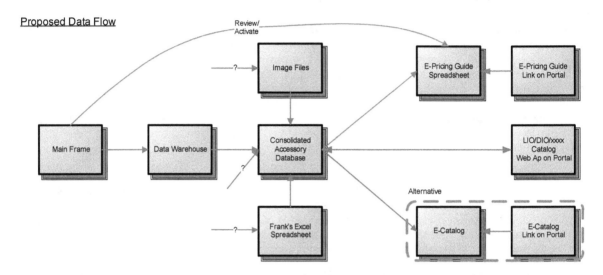

I mentioned at the end of the first two sections that what we reported is the end result of investigation, interactions, and interviews. We are telling the story of what we have learned and validated together. I state this simple concept again because it is important. Anyone closely involved should be able to tell the story using the A3 as a simple guide. The A3 report cannot be written in advance of the collaborative work required to learn and gain agreement. At this point, we presented the proposal to the Director of Marketing. The solution set was accepted with very little additional discussion, even though it was very different from what he had initially envisioned.

Facilitation Tip: Dialog then Discussion (Senge)

Understanding and practicing dialog then discussion fosters team work and leads to better decisions. The purpose of discussion is to win, to decide, to have one's view accepted by the group. This form of interaction is prevalent especially in business. The purpose of dialog is learning by sharing many points of view to access a "pool of common understanding." Reflection and inquiry are necessary skills to support dialog. Dialog is a team sport. These are distinctly different interactions and likely need to be intentionally facilitated.

Conditions for Dialog

- All participants must suspend their assumptions.
- All participants must regard themselves as colleagues.
- There must be a facilitator who holds the context of the dialog.

In our case, we intentionally practiced dialog while brainstorming and evaluating potential solutions. We resorted to discussion to decide on our proposed solutions sets. Dialog then discussion occurred during analysis as well. We brainstormed potential causes then decided which causes needed to be addressed most urgently. Both are valuable. Dialog is harder.

Facilitation Tip: Set-Based Decision Making
The A3 process promotes set-based decision making. Characteristics include generate multiple options, consider blending potential solutions, experiment and learn, and delay critical decisions until the right time. This practice generates better results.

Thinking Element: Coherency
The completed A3 report presents a coherent storyline that explains why we are taking this improvement action. It shows a logical flow of thinking from organizational goals to the problem to the solution. A good A3 report makes the approach and context visible to ensure key thinking is included and implementation is progressing.

A3 Process Step 4: Action Plan
The final part of the A3 report is to plan the action and follow-up. At the conclusion of the project planning we had actually already started work on the solutions. We knew what to do. But would we remember who committed to do what by when in a week, a month, a few months? My recommendation is to list the deliverables or expected results. Include a few details about the expected outcome. Include columns for the person responsible, the completion date, and the reviewer to verify completion. Include at least one follow up item to check that progress was made towards the opportunity/problem statement or that the goal was achieved (if you have one). Here is my recommended format.

Action Plan (deliverables or tasks for selected solutions)

Step	Deliverable	Pulled by	Date Pulled	Reviewer
1.				
2.				
3.				
4.				
5.				
6.				

Follow Up (Check that Goal was met)

In our case, the project was actually planned in MS Project in more detail than was probably necessary. Here is what we included on the A3 report.

INVOLVE & EMPOWER EMPLOYEES

Partner a developer, an analyst, and an additional business resource with Kevin to automate product information management and convert data to the new process

CONTINUOUSLY IMPROVE

Show the team what has been accomplished

CONCLUSION: PULL-BASED AUTHORITY

The A3 process is also a management training and learning approach. It provides guidance to ask the right questions and get superior results. Teams and individuals can earn the authority to be empowered through competently practicing A3 thinking. Characteristics include demonstrating solid problem solving and collaboration skills, delivering performance results, and being trustworthy.

REFERENCES

Deming, W. E. (2000). *The New Economics for Industry, Government, Education 2nd edition*. Cambridge, MA: First MIT Press.

Merifeld, R. & Calhoun, J., & Stevens, Dennis, (2008). *The Next Revolution in Productivity*. Retrieved 6 June, 2008 from www.hbr.org.

Senge, P. (1990). *The Fifth Discipline: The Art and Practice of the Learning Organization*. New York, NY: Currency Books.

Sobek, D.K. & Smalley, A. (2008). *Understanding A3 Thinking: A Critical Component of Toyota's PDCA Management System*. Boca Raton, FL: Productivity Press.

Shook, J. (2009). *Managing to Learn: Using A3 management process to solve problems, gain agreement, mentor, and lead*. Cambridge, MA. Lean Enterprise Institute, Inc.

The Standish Group Internationnal, Inc. (2009). *Chaos Summary 2009*. Retrived 18 December, 2010 from http://www1.standishgroup.com/newsroom/chaos_2009.php

Improve e-Pricing Guide & Accessory Catalogs

SPECIFY VALUE IN THE EYES OF THE CUSTOMER
Consolidated catalog including LIO/DIO with accurate and
complete information to facilitate the sales process .

As Is Data Flow

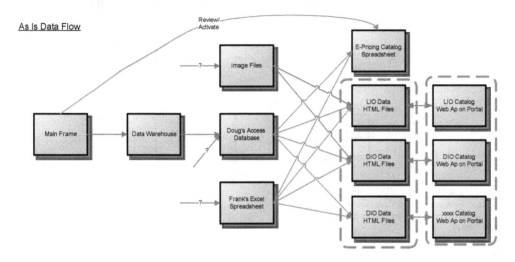

IDENTIFY WASTE: Lines in red indicate waste.
1. Manual work that takes more time than necessary and results in
errors and missing information.
2. HTML files difficult to manage automatically. Review of
information problematic.
3. Multiple catalogs cause dealer associates to toggle between LIO
and DIO to gather information for customers . Customer desires
one place to find all accessories for a model.

ELIMINATE WASTE:
1. Consolidate accessory information into one database. This
eliminates to need to manually update a variety of HTML files .
2. Eliminate HTML interface and pull information directly from the
consolidated database.

FLOW WHERE YOU CAN, PULL WHERE YOU MUST

Proposed Data Flow

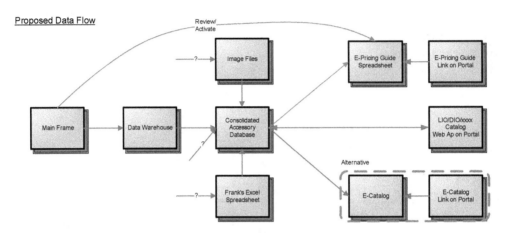

INVOLVE & EMPOWER EMPLOYEES
Partner a developer, an analyst, and an additional business
resource with Kevin to automate product information management
and convert data to the new process

CONTINUOUSLY IMPROVE
Show the team what has been accomplished

Lean Systems Engineering within System Design Activities

by

Richard Turner, DSc   richard.turner@stevens.edu

Jon Wade, PhD   jon.wade@stevens.edu

ABSTRACT

Design within Systems Engineering (SE) in its traditional form is primarily a hierarchical decomposition of system requirements into a variety of architectural components (e.g. functional architecture, physical architecture, allocated architecture, interface structure). As systems become more complex and requirements less tangible, more evolving, and sometimes emergent, this hierarchical approach has become more difficult. Agile and lean engineering principles developed to address non-determinism in software systems involve iterative and spiral concepts, generally use less traditional ceremony, and require closer interaction with stakeholders. This paper discusses how these principles may be practically applied in performing SE activities during the design of complex or evolving hardware-software-human systems.

INTRODUCTION

Traditional systems engineering (SE) was developed around half a century ago, primarily driven by the challenges faced in the aerospace and defense industries.   The context for this discipline was fairly uniform, with the result being that practices that were successful in this environment were generally seen as "best practices" and came to define the discipline of SE. These practices have evolved based on their legacy roots, and so today's SE still looks and feels similar to the discipline applied within that 1960s aerospace and defense context. Current SE maintains a process/practice standpoint. It can be characterized by:

- a defined, deterministic life cycle guiding the application of various tools and techniques.

- checklists of work products.

- a focus on integrating and managing the structured execution of processes by multiple, different types of engineering toward the development of a specific system.

Design within systems engineering is typically hierarchical in nature and based on functional or equipment boundaries. This is a valid and proven approach, and has worked well — up to a point. The environment and context for system development has changed dramatically over the last decade or two, and the practice of systems engineering has simply not kept pace. Software-driven, net centric solutions, the rise of complex heterogeneous systems of systems, and the near ubiquitous availability of exponentially improving computing power, storage capacity, and communication bandwidth have all had a significant impact. However, the common factor of all these technologies is that they either enable or depend upon increasing amounts of critical software. This prevalence of software in systems has been a major impact on SE: the inherent flexibility it provides, its criticality to nearly every system function, and the non-deterministic aspects of its development. Those characteristics are key drivers that led to agile and lean software development paradigms.

AGILE AND LEAN APPROACHES

There are many agile techniques and a broad set of lean-based philosophies extant in today's engineering world. Agile is seen primarily in software activities and lean in manufacturing. This is changing as we understand more about the actual impacts of the various practices on the underlying aspects of developing products. It is becoming easier to see that these concepts are much more universal than first thought, leading us to the questions about applying the concepts to a broader set of disciplines. One example is the use of agile concepts in crisis management (Harrald 2004).

In my research, I am looking for ways to "lighten the ceremony" and make systems engineering practice more amenable in fast-paced or complex development environments such as defense, the intelligence community, and health care. While every agile or lean practice may not be applicable to systems engineering and system design, we can apply the key lean and agile principles. Since there are so many different characterizations of agile and lean, I have provided my personal list of the key principles I believe most likely to be applicable to systems engineering. These are drawn from my experiences and have been influenced by Reinertsen (1997), Anderson (2010), and Boehm (2004) among others.

Key agile principles

- Planning-driven, not plan-driven
- Evidence-based progress assessment
- Short iterations/short learning cycle
- Continuous integration and testing
- Continuous stakeholder involvement
- Early value to the customer

Key lean principles

- Reduced work in progress
- Small batch sizes
- Incorporation of cost of delay and value of information in planning
- Defer decisions until the latest reasonable time
- Flow (queue) management

SYSTEM DESIGN WITHIN SYSTEMS ENGINEERING

Buede (2009) defines System Design within SE as a set of six repetitive and concurrent functions:

1.   Define the system level design problem being solved.

2.   Develop the system functional architecture.

3.   Develop the system physical architecture.

4.   Develop the system allocated architecture.

5.   Develop the system interface architecture.

6.   Define the qualification system for the system.

Without going deeply into the specific activities of these functions, we can summarize in the following way: make sure that you understand what the system you are designing needs to do, that you develop a number of architectural components that describe how the product will be built to do what it needs to do, and then describe the system to make sure that the product, once built, indeed does what it needs to do. Essentially, then, we are looking at three key activities: requirements, architecture, and validation.

AGILE AND LEAN ENGINEERING APPROACHES WITHIN SYSTEM DESIGN
Probably the most difficult issue with systems engineering in modern systems is applying what has traditionally been a generally sequential process to an environment that forces more and more concurrency. This results from several factors, including the compression of schedules to meet customer demands or impending threats, the rapid evolution of technology and available components, and evolving systems interacting with legacy systems that were never designed to act as anything but stand alone solutions. The following sections provide examples of cases where lean and agile principles can be implemented within the three key activities noted earlier, with only some impact on traditional processes.

Requirements
Requirements have been near the top of the list of software and systems engineering issues (NDIA 2003, 2006, 2010) for years. In large complex systems and rapid developments, requirements pose similar but strikingly different problems. In a complex system, particularly one with long-lead items, requirements need to be carefully engineered and specified as early as possible to prevent changes rippling through and negating or delaying expensive research, development, and manufacturing activities. In a rapid environment, the requirements need to be brief enough that work can begin as soon as possible to be able to meet sometimes immovable deadlines. Rapid deployment fits the agile home ground. Large complex system developers have primarily allocated agile approaches to support subsystems or small specialized functionality, such as mission loading devices for aircraft or GUI development. There are, however, other ways in which lean and agile approaches impact requirements even in the largest of systems. Two areas where requirements could benefit from agile and lean principles are described below.

Stakeholder involvement
Probably the most important stakeholder role, after funding, is as a source for requirements. The agile principle that stakeholders should be continuously involved is one way to

ensure that the requirements don't change so radically that work is lost, that the requirements are in fact achievable given the resources, and that requirements can be prioritized to support iterative or evolutionary development paradigms. The right stakeholders are critical. As stated in Boehm (2004), involved stakeholders "should be CRACK performers: Collaborative, Representative, Authorized, Committed, and Knowledgeable. Shortfalls in any of these capabilities can lead to frustration, delay, and wasted project effort, not to mention a non-acceptable product."

Modeling

One means of maintaining requirements stability, or at least managing changes, is through modeling. Modeling is a valid form of evidence-based progress assessment and can provide huge benefits to the stakeholders and the developers in creating, evaluating, and continuously managing requirements. From early models of the concept of operations to validate and prioritize requirements, to models that support engineering or requirements trade-offs under budget stresses, to those used to support validation, fielding, and training, models can be well worth the investment.

Within the lean principles, the value of the information gathered in modeling, particularly if done early, is extremely high because it allows failure with low rework costs (Reinertsen 1997). Financial as well as technical modeling based on the value of the various requirements — even lower level specifications — can also help in queue management (Reinertsen 1997) by establishing and adjusting correct work in progress limits and levels of service in kanban queues (Andersen 2010).

Architecture

Four of the six design tasks from Buede are architecture-related. Obviously, defining and managing the architecture(s) are the most significant activities in system design. The architectural components enable realization of the functional requirements, and are the sole means of achieving cross-cutting non-functional attributes such as safety, security, and availability.

Because of the simple design principle introduced in extreme programming and associated with the acronym YAGNI (You Aren't Going to Need It), agile approaches have been labeled as anti-architecture. As agile approaches have been scaled to address larger systems, however, the concept of simple design has been relaxed into a more Einstein-like rule of "Everything as simple as possible, but not simpler." Lean philosophy, on the other hand, sees architecture as a critical cost trade-off as well as an enabler for deferring decisions, adding customer value inexpensively later, supporting product lines, and handling changes. The following are two examples of areas where architecture development could benefit from agile/ lean principles.

Managing variability

In (Boehm 2004) and (Reinertsen 1997), there is a preferred approach of having the architecture isolate those aspects that are most vulnerable to change such that changes will not ripple through the system as a whole. Eberhardt Rechtin states this as a heuristic "Design the elements to make their performance as insensitive to unknown or uncontrollable external influences as practical" (Rechtin 1991). Where there needs to be a long life cycle, the best architectures are those that evolve gracefully and have the fewest vulnerabilities to "architecture-busting" issues arising from foreseeable change.

Learning, iterations, and work-in-progress

Another of Rechtin's heuristics is "Don't assume that the original statement of the problem is necessarily the best, or even the right, one." While generally applied to requirements, it states a key concept in systems design: there is a learning process associated with building complex systems of any sort. And, the more times we fail, the more we learn (up to a point). Iterations of architectural products seem very appropriate for learning about systems. Unlike defects in an implementation, though, defects in an architecture are much more difficult to identify. Cost, performance, and longevity issues are all related to architectural decisions. The Software Engineering Institute (SEI) at Carnegie Mellon University has done groundbreaking work in software and software system architectures. SEI has developed approaches to evaluate architectures and architectural trade-off decisions based on the system's required quality attributes (Kazman 2000, Clements 2000, Asundi 2001).

By combining the use of iterations, SEI or other architectural evaluation methods, and value models such as Reinertsen's financial modeling, it seems possible to measure the impact of changes or additions to the architecture in each iteration against architectural and financial goals. Managing the iterations of architectural work must, however, be included in the queuing and work in progress decisions of all development activities and may need special levels of service when being conducted concurrently with other work.

Validation

Applying agile and lean concepts to the validation of systems design does not pose as many conceptual problems as its application to requirements and architecture, but it does impact the practical aspects within traditional validation approaches. The following are two examples of agile/lean approaches that can support validation.

Continuous validation

Both agile and lean principles lead to practices for continuous validation. As system engineering continues to develop architectural products, and as those are designed and implemented, maintaining some form of testing and integration cycles is valuable in identifying specification and architectural flaws such as interface mismatches, as well as a means to evaluate the impact of changes. Frequent validation activities also reduce batch sizes and work-in-progress in the validation efforts, leading to more efficiency and better flow.

Testing Efficiency

Using the value of information, the Pareto 80/20 principle, and cost of delay, it is possible to reduce the amount of testing needed to produce the needed quality. Examples of this type of analysis are provided in both Boehm (2005) and Reinertsen (1997). Figure 1, from the Boehm example, compares the cost of using a value-based Pareto approach versus a value-neutral automatic test generation tool. It shows that while the tool provides a benefit at the end, the

Pareto approach results in a much higher return on investment at only 40% of the tests. This suggests that making intelligent decisions about what to test can lead to a much better testing return on investment.

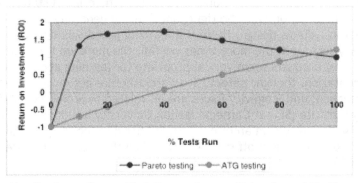

Figure 1. Comparative Business Cases: Test Generator vs. Value-based Testing

CONCLUSION

Given the difficulty in applying lean and agile approaches to traditionally sequential processes, the examples provided here bode well for a more complete investigation. While certainly not exhaustive, nor described in sufficient detail to be formulaically applied, determined practitioners can find ways to implement these approaches into existing processes, and hopefully provide additional guidance and empirical information on their performance. The practices also represent a starting place for more complete rethinking of systems engineering and how it can adjust to a more concurrent and rapidly changing environment.

REFERENCES

Anderson, David. (2010). *Kanban: Successful Evolutionary Change for Your Technology Business.* Sequim, WA: Blue Hole Press

Asundi, Jay, et al (2001). *Using Economic Considerations to Choose Among Architecture Design Alternatives.* TECHNICAL REPORT 2001-TR-035, Software Engineering Institute, Carnegie Mellon University, December, 2001.

Basili, Victor R., Boehm, Barry (2001) "Software Defect Reduction Top 10 List," Computer, January 2001, pp. 135-137.

Boehm, Barry and Turner, Richard (2004). *Balancing Agility and Discipline: A Guide for the Perplexed.* Boston, MA: Addison Wesley.

Boehm, Barry (2005). *Value-Based Software Engineering: Overview and Agenda.* University of Southern California Center for Software Engineering Technical Report USC-CSE-2005-504. Los Angeles, CA: USC CSE, February 2005.

Buede, Dennis M. (2009). *The Engineering Design of Systems: Models and Methods.* Hoboken, NJ: John Wiley and Sons.

Clements, Paul, et al (2001). *Evaluating Software Architectures: Methods and Case Studies.* Boston, MA: Addison Wesley.

Harrald, John. (2006) "Agility and Discipline: Critical Success Factors for Disaster Response," The ANNALS of the American Academy of Political and Social Science. March 2006 vol. 604 no. 1, pp. 256-272

Kazman, Rick, et al (2000). ATAM: Method for Architecture Evaluation, TECHNICAL REPORT CMU/ SEI-2000-TR-004, Software Engineering Institute, Carnegie Mellon University, August, 2000.

NDIA-National Defense Industrial Association (2010). *Top Systems Engineering Issues In US Defense Industry.* Systems Engineering Division Task Group Report, http://www.ndia.org/Divisions/ Divisions/SystemsEngineering/Documents/Studies/Top%20SE%20Issues%202010%20Report%20 v11%20FINAL.pdf. September, 2010.

NDIA-National Defense Industrial Association (2006). *Top Five Systems Engineering Issues within Department of Defense and Defense Industry.* Systems Engineering Division Task Group Report, http://www.ndia.org/Divisions/Divisions/SystemsEngineering/Documents/Studies/NDIA%20 Top5%20SE%20Issues%202006%20Report%20v8%20final.pdf. July, 2006.

NDIA-National Defense Industrial Association (2003). *Top Five Systems Engineering Issues In Defense Industry.* Systems Engineering Division Task Group Report http://www.aticourses.com/

sampler/TopFiveSystemsEngineeringIssues_In_DefenseIndustry.pdf. January, 2003.

Rechtin, Eberhardt (1991). *Systems Architecting: Creating and Building Complex Systems*. Englewood Cliffs, NJ: Prentice Hall PTR.

Reinertsen, Donald G. (1997). *Managing the Design Factory: A Product Developer's Toolkit*. New York: The Free Press.

Using Flow Approaches to Effectively Manage Agile Testing

by

Yuval Yeret, Yuval@AgileSparks.com

ABSTRACT

This paper will focus on improving agility in complex environments, where it is not realistic to finish all required work, and especially testing work, within one sprint, so classic agile iterations fall short. This paper will introduce a more generic flow-based recipe for these environments. I will outline techniques for visualizing and reducing testing batch sizes within sprints/releases using Cumulative Flow Diagrams (CFD), discuss how to deal with the testing bottleneck that is so common in product development organizations, and discuss how to deal with policies rooted in the current big batch approach to product development.

INTRODUCTION

A rapidly increasing amount of organizations want to become more agile these days. Several field case studies show that when an enterprise-level organization undertakes this endeavor, it ends up having a significant stabilization/hardening phase, usually in the order of 30% of the effort and schedule of the whole release. This is a result of the high transaction costs associated with running testing cycles, aiming to locally optimize the testing efficiency by reducing the number of cycles and the pursuit of scale economy. The lean/kanban practitioner will be worried by this point, and will not be surprised to learn that a lot of waste, ineffective handoffs, and mountains of rework usually ensue. The result is typically low predictability as to whether this stabilization phase ends on time and whether the end result will be in release-level quality. This is the culmination of the big batch thinking that is inherent to traditional software development approaches. It also drives a destructive cycle of longer and longer stabilization phases when we see we cannot deliver quality on time. We set a policy of longer stabilization feature freeze. We have less time to actually develop so we run an even faster and more reckless development cycle.

Testing is deemed more and more expensive, so we try to make it more efficient by running less and less cycles. Integration is deemed expensive and problematic, so we set a policy of integration just after the parts are complete and in high quality, while forgetting that the real quality challenges of the day are the integration aspects, which should be dealt with as early as possible.

GOING AGILE ALL THE WAY

When such an organization starts the move to agile, several scenarios can materialize. The ideal alternative is for agile teams to take on all of the stabilization work as part of their definition of done and deliver working, tested software that is release ready within each increment/iteration/sprint. Furthermore, accompanied with massive test automation, this minimizes the regression/stabilization cycle effort, and the stabilization phase can be expected to shrink dramatically.

AGILE IN COMPLEX ENVIRONMENTS

Another scenario happens in more complex environments. When moving to full-scale agile teams, the regression effort and the scope of testing coverage required are still extremely high, making it an impossible endeavor for the agile team to solve the problem as easily as before. First, it is not always feasible to complete all the required testing work on a story within a sprint. Second, even if it is possible, ensuring no regression impact due to those stories is a transaction cost that is either not feasible or not economically reasonable. Third, sometimes the work required to take a story to release-level quality is again more than a sprint can contain. Aspects like Enterprise-Readiness, Performance, and Security, applied to a big legacy system, require specialized approaches, special skills, labs, and time. Typically the agile team runs at a certain pace, delivering a certain level of working and tested software. Then there is a process outside the team of taking that software and making it release quality. The focus of this work is to assist organizations in managing this complex process, applying lean/agile principles of product development flow in order to reduce the overall price of quality and improve the overall predictability.

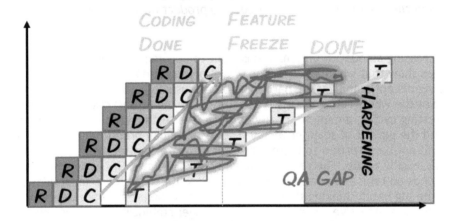

Figure 1. Testing Gaps in Complex Agile Environments

A MORE EVOLUTIONARY APPROACH TO AGILITY

Another scenario is the organizations that want to improve their development processes using a more evolutionary approach (Anderson 2010). In this context, the concept of an agile team doesn't even necessarily exist, so the level of "doneness" of work is even lower at the outset.

LOOKING FOR A SPECIFIC SOLUTION TO ESCALATING RELEASE COSTS

Lastly, we see several organizations that are looking specifically for a solution to this problem. They are not looking to become more agile per se but they are focused on reducing the cost of releasing and improving their due date performance. Yes, they see that it will allow shorter releases and better maneuverability, but it is a secondary side benefit for them.

IMPROVING STABILIZATION IN COMPLEX SCENARIOS

This paper will present a recipe that can be applied to these scenarios in order to reduce the cost of stabilization while improving its predictability by applying the principles of agility and flow without assuming full team-level agility and engineering practices.

I want to emphasize the last point. The typical agile practitioner will claim that all of this headache can be resolved by going on the agile diet, that extreme programming accompanied by a strict pure Scrum process will resolve all of the problems. I tend to agree. But not all organizations want to (or can) go on this extreme "diet." Not all of them can afford the change on a short time frame, and even worse, at the higher levels of complexity and enterprise scale, agile would certainly help but it would not be enough to resolve the problem completely. As the reader will see later on, the recipe includes certain key practices from the agile diet, albeit in a form that can be adopted as part of an evolutionary process.

IDENTIFYING A GOOD SOLUTION

How will we know we have a good solution for our problem? We will have to improve in two key aspects. The first is to achieve a major reduction in the length of the stabilization/hardening phase. The second is to dramatically improve the predictability of the release due date while still meeting the release criteria.

WHAT CAUSES THE PROBLEM

Let us start our journey towards a solution by understanding what the root causes of the problem are. Figure 2 shows a current reality tree (Dettmer 1998) that helps us understand the cause and effect relationships.

Why is stabilization cost so high? Mainly because we get late feedback on our decisions, and we know that late quality is more expensive quality. Why do we get late feedback? Because we prefer to work in big batches due to high costs of every stabilization cycle and since we believe it is the efficient and right way to do things. We believe we cannot really achieve good coverage and certainty about the quality of the release without running a big batch once everything is ready. In addition, sometimes features aren't ready for feedback until late in the cycle. Why? Sometimes it is because they are big features. Another reason is that we are not focusing on just a few features; we are working on many features in parallel (feature per engineer sometimes) which means they will take a lot of calendar time due to excessive multi-tasking at the organization level. Note that even if each engineer/team is single-tasking, if we are multiplexing stories/work from various features, then at the organization/release level we are still multi-tasking. (Why, by the way, do we typically see many features in progress? We tend to believe it is more efficient, minimizes coordination overhead, gives more ownership to the Feature Owner, and many engineers prefer to run solo.)

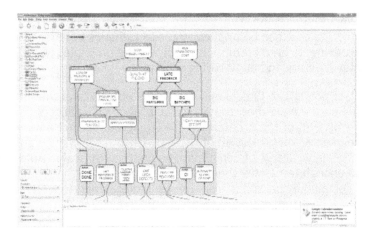

Figure 2. Current Reality of Stabilization Costs

All this means quality is "added" after the fact. As documented in Capers Jones Cost of Quality (1980), the later we find and deal with defects the more expensive it becomes. Late quality is expensive.

With this dynamic in place, we have two options: protect the quality and compromise on due date performance or protect the due date and compromise on quality, whether explicit or implicit. The team is driven hard, way beyond sustainable pace, and they find the ways to "make ends meet." Bugs are ignored, quick and dirty local fixes are applied, etc. This increases the lack of predictability of how this saga will end and when.

WORKING TOWARDS A SOLUTION

So what do we do about the problem? One option we discussed before is to go agile all the way. We will not outline the details of this solution here to maintain brevity. Note though that even in some agile team scenarios leftovers of untested unfinished work will accumulate after each sprint. Beyond high stabilization costs, sometimes the gap grows to such an extent that there is no option but to throw away features that were already developed once it is understood there is no way to test them in the release. When this happens, the morale of the team sinks. We usually see it happening around the time the developers are asked to go help the testers deal with the remaining features that are not trashed.

In addition, there is typically a drive towards developing functionality as fast as possible and leaving defects for later. This policy makes sense when a feature freeze phase is mandated. The main thing the developers can do during this period is fix defects. If you fix defects earlier, you deliver less functionality until feature freeze. If you CAN defer defect fixing to after the feature freeze cutoff date, this is what you will do. This problem exists even in some agile teams.

DONE IS DONE

The first step towards a solution is to consider a feature as «Done» only if it is completely finished and can pass its release-grade criteria. This means it has passed all of its test coverage, and all the defects that need to be fixed and verified to pass release grade criteria have been dealt with. (For project management purposes we will track which features are done, and which are still in progress.) The important point to note is that even if stories or aspects of this feature have been completed in an agile team, the feature itself will be considered just work in progress.

LIMITING FEATURES IN PROGRESS

Next, limit the amount of features that can be in progress. Allow the starting of a new feature only if a previous one is really finished and release ready and the amount of open defects is below a certain low threshold. This limit synchronizes the project. However, it doesn't require the extreme synchronization that happens inside an agile team.

DEALING WITH THE TESTING BOTTLENECK AT THE TACTICAL LEVEL

Developers will be asked to optimize features reaching Done rather than features reaching Coded. This might mean investing more in quality at the coder level (automated unit tests come to mind), reducing the number of defects delivered with the code by doing code reviews or pair programming, etc. Readers familiar with the Theory of Constraints will recognize this as exploiting the testing constraint, exploit being one of the five focusing steps (Coxx and Goldratt 1986).

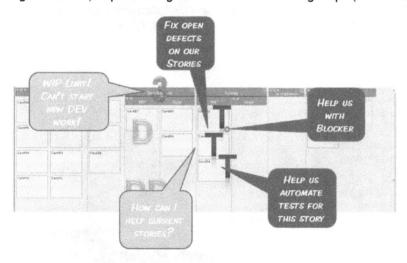

Figure 3. What developers can do during an active testing bottleneck

AVOIDING THE DANGERS OF BOTTLENECKS

In many cases, even after increasing quality of Coded features, a testing gap will still be apparent. Are we really asking developers to slow down and avoid coding new features? This might lead to lost capacity in the release and to lower capabilities over time if the developers "forget how to run fast" (Anderson 2004). We want to avoid this. Instead, let's identify work types that don't need to go through the bottleneck or that require less capacity from it. Choose work that is not testing-heavy, or items that can be tested without the involvement of the testing bottleneck. This introduces an internal operations factor into the priority filter, but clearly this optimizes for overall business value outcome.

INVESTING TO ELEVATE BOTTLENECKS

To elevate a testing bottleneck, create a backlog of engineering investments that will improve testing capacity, usually by reducing the amount of work needed per feature. The best example is, of course, test automation that can conveniently also be developed by developers. This backlog solves the slow down problem. It also is a more sensitive solution than "Have slack in the system" to the slack created by sprint commitment and limited WIP. Involve your teams in building the Engineering Investment backlogs to increase their commitment to this approach. Experience also shows that higher commitment exists when working to elevate rather than locally deal with a problem.

THE TEST AUTOMATION PYRAMID HELPS ELEVATING BOTTLENECKS

In the context of testing, leverage the recommendation of the "Test Automation Pyramid" (Crispin and Gregory 2009) to achieve a win-win: Reduce the cost of test automation by doing more of it in layers that are cheaper to maintain, like unit testing and service/api-level testing rather than at the UI level, and benefit from the fact that these layers are closer to the comfort zone of the developers. Extend the "Pyramid" to all of the testing aspects required to get a feature to release-ready. Considering this work as part of the flow/bottleneck optimization picture is key to achieving lower stabilization costs and better release flows. Consider this a form of "Continuous Stabilization" or "Continuous Hardening".

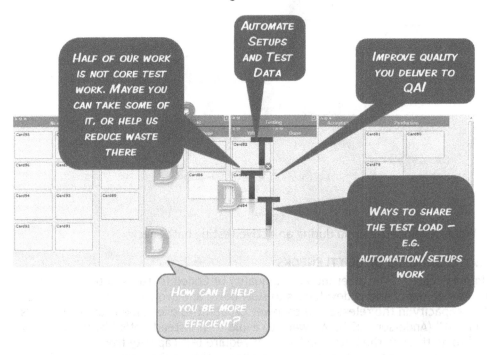

Figure 4. What developers can do to elevate a testing bottleneck

SAFELY TRANSITIONING TO A SHORTER STABILIZATION PERIOD

Finally, choose when to go into stabilization (and stop developing new features) based on metrics presented earlier. If the number of open defects is low, and there is a low amount of feature work in progress, it might be safe to proceed further with new features. If defects are mounting, and lots of features are in progress, risk is high, and it is best to aim for stabilization as quickly as possible, or at least to stop the line, reduce the work in progress, and then reconsider.

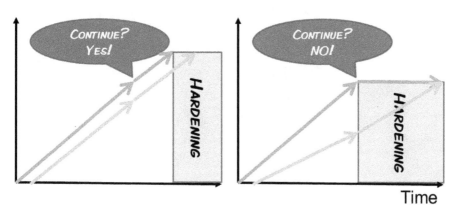

Figure 5. Dynamic decision to go into hardening phase

CONCLUSION

To summarize, in many product development scenarios, whether agile or not, escalating stabilization costs are a painful problem in need of a solution. Lean/agile approaches can help reduce the problem. We outlined a solution relying on an end-to-end pragmatic approach that doesn't require a revolution in the way the product is developed, instead driving an evolutionary focused improvement by tying all the parts together and aiming at global optimization. This solution can be applied in the field as part of agile implementation projects, on a standalone basis, or as a preamble that will drive the understanding that a more agile approach needs to be adopted as a way to improve on the bottlenecks identified by this method.

REFERENCES

Anderson, D. (2004). Four Roles of Agile Management. *Cutter IT Journal*. Retrieved 10 March 2011 from http://www.agilemanagement.net/AMPDFArchive/FourRolesFinalRev0804.pdf

Anderson, D. (2010). *Kanban*. Sequim, WA: Blue Hole Press.

Crispin, L. & Gregory, J. (2009). *Agile Testing: A Practical Guide for Testers and Agile Teams*. Reading, MA: Addison-Wesley Professional.

Dettmer, H. W. (1998). *Breaking the constraints to world class performance*. Milwaukee, WI: ASQ Quality Press.

Goldratt, E. M. & Coxx, J.(1986). *The goal: a process of ongoing improvement*. Great Barrington, MA: North River Press.

Jones, C. (2008) *Applied Software Measurement, 3rd edition*. New York, NY: McGraw Hill.

Reinertsen, D. (2009). *The Principles of Product Development Flow: Second Generation Lean Product Development*. Redondo Beach, CA: Celeritas Publishing.

Innovation as a Science:

General Theory of Innovation (GTI) and Its Applications to Growth,

Competitive Advantage, and Development of Successful Innovations

by

Greg Yezersky, gyezersky@strategicinnovation.com

ABSTRACT

Innovation is an essential business function and the foundation of market success, but it is an elusive target. The data shows that the odds of creating a profitable new market offering are below 25% (a study by Harvard and Deloitte), and the odds of generating growth are below 1% (a study by Frost & Sullivan).

This situation has drastically changed with the emergence of the General Theory of Innovation (GTI). GTI posits that it is possible to create meaningful and unique innovations virtually on demand that would lead to sustainable competitive advantage and growth. With its structured perspective, GTI is a universal approach that can be applied to any organization or enterprise, and to any market, and is directly relevant to the LeanSSC mission and objectives.

INTRODUCTION: WHY IS A SCIENTIFIC THEORY OF INNOVATION THE IMPERATIVE?

The nature of success in the business world is almost self-obvious. The company that creates a greater value for its respective market will prosper, while the competitors will only get what is left for them by the leader. Repeat creating this difference in value year after year, and success will be permanently associated with you and your organization. It seems so simple, but is it?

CHALLENGE: THE KEY PROBLEM OF THE BUSINESS WORLD AND RELATED FACTS

All the entities seek to sustain the growth that initially put them on the world's business map, but no one ever has been able to achieve it. Stats are horrific.

According to a study conducted by Royal Dutch Shell [1], the average life expectancy of Fortune 500 firms is 40 to 50 years! The time of being a market leader is even shorter. Thus, the leaders continue rising and falling. The names of Kmart, AOL, GM, Morgan Stanley, Lehman Brothers, AIG, Enron, and many others easily come to mind. Examples of failures abound; they are so overwhelming that after studying the history of business, professors W. Chan Kim and Renee Mauborgne (INSEAD) wrote: "...permanently excellent industries and companies do not exist." [2]

Everyone recognizes that innovation is the ultimate remedy for this challenge, but it is elusive and extremely risky. According to a study by Harvard and Deloitte [3], the odds of an innovation to generate profit do not exceed 24 percent, while the odds of an innovation to create growth [4] are below 1%. No firm can continually beat these odds, hence every company eventually ceases to grow, and the majority die even though they are at least theoretically immortal.

This paper sequentially presents the following questions and answers:

- Why are the odds so small? It pinpoints the Root Cause that determines the risks.
- With literally hundreds of innovation approaches and techniques available, why can't they meaningfully improve the above odds?
- What is the only way that the challenge can be addressed? The scientific theory, General Theory of Innovation (GTI), and its fundamentals will be introduced.
- The paper also presents GTI major capabilities and the range of applications.

The key problem analysis: the root cause of growth

Figure 1. The process of innovation and its major stages

Regardless of whether innovators realize it or not, creating an innovation is a process (Figure 1) that consists of five major stages: identification of market requirements for a future product (service); formulation of problems that need to be solved to meet the requirements; analysis and solution of the problems; solutions evaluation that also includes identification of potential consequences (both positive and negative) resulting from a planned change; and, finally, formulation of the future Value Proposition concept, which is the foundation for the rest of the production cycle. Depending on how sound the foundation is, the cycle results will vary greatly.

Even quick analysis of the process clearly shows that we do not control it well. For example, the enterprises do not have reliable methods to identify the future of the market's needs accurately, which makes control over the entire process of innovation impossible in principle. The same is true for the rest of the stages. Even if we optimistically assign a 50/50 probability of having a successful outcome to each of the stages, the overall process success odds do not exceed 3%, and we have not even started the development yet.

Since the entire chain is as strong as its weakest link, our inability to control the process of innovation, the first stage, automatically leads to the situation where no company can control the results of competition. This, in turn, results in a company's inability to succeed continuously and, ultimately, control its own destiny. The inability to control the process of innovation is the Root Cause behind the cessation of growth, market losses, and eventual mortality of the business enterprises.

The need for the science of innovation - the definitive remedy

To overcome the Root Cause of growth cessation and make innovation more manageable, any methodology or approach MUST satisfy the following criteria:

- Effectiveness (how good the results are)
- Efficiency (how many resources a process consumes and how much of each)
- Robustness (consistency of results from one project to another project)
- Reproducibility of results (by other people - user independent)
- Transferability of knowledge about a methodology to other people
- Range of applications or issues that a methodology addresses

When one applies this set of criteria to all the available methodologies, the majority of them do not satisfy even half of these criteria, as they do not control the process of innovation, including identification of future customers' needs.

There is only one reliable method to control any kind of activity known to humanity, namely, through the creation and use of science. Science allows us to significantly improve our problem-solving capabilities, our forecasting capabilities, and our objective judgment capabilities regardless of the area of application. It enables better control of risk, more effective management, and results that are more consistent.

For example, while many believe that the future is unknowable, due to the existence of physics, we can bet (with great results) that a glass cup falling from a table will hit the ground. Moreover, by knowing the table height, we can predict when it will hit the ground. Finally, by knowing the ground properties, we can reliably predict whether the cup will break or survive the fall.

With all of the above in mind, there is no adequate substitute for a science of innovation. We state with confidence that as long as the entities will use any other approach to innovation, they will rise and fall, and the rate of failure will remain unacceptably high.

THE GENERAL THEORY OF INNOVATION (GTI)

Guided by the above requirements, the author of this paper embarked on the road to create a theory satisfying them, which a few years later (1992) resulted in the creation of the theory that is now known as the General Theory of Innovation (GTI).

The research approach

Right from the start, three crucial choices were made. First, instead of studying the working of the mind, which is not well understood and is subjective, the focus was on studying the objective evolutionary process of real-world systems: products, processes, services, companies, markets. Second, the systems were deliberately chosen of different nature, both technology-based and not technology-based. Finally, the investigation focused on both the systems themselves and (mostly!) on the relationships the systems had with their respective Environments. This means that the investigation wanted to uncover the driving forces behind the process of evolution, including identifying those factors that cause the need for innovations/solutions as well as those conditions that caused emergence of the problems and determined subsequent success or failure of the proposed solutions. Here are a few examples of the systems that were investigated:

- Sound storage medium has evolved from Edison's phonograph to wax cylinders, to discs with lateral grooves, to double-sided discs, to reel-to-reel magnetic tapes, to 4- and 8-track tape cartridges, to compact cassettes, to CD, to DVD, to MP3.[5]

- The use of currency evolved from the barter of goods (cattle, grain, etc.) to silver ingots guaranteed by Cappadocian rulers (2200 BC), to the first crude coins made from naturally occurring amalgam of gold and silver (640 BC), to Chinese paper money (800 AD), to bank-backed notes (1633-1660), to the first credit card (1950s), to electronic money.[6]
- Message delivery evolved from sending a messenger on foot to a messenger on horseback, to the creation of regular mail service, to mail service supported by cars, trains, and planes, to fax, to the next day service, to e-mail.

Major findings and conclusions

Despite being very different, innovations have a number of things in common.

- **Any product or service (process) is a system.**
  This means that every product or service represents a union of parts or procedures connected to each other in order to deliver value to the customers. No individual element of a system can deliver the same value on its own.

- **Systems (products, services, industries) evolve.**
  Systems evolve over time to adapt to changes in customers' needs and desires.

- **Superiority of problems: problems are more important than solutions.**
  The analysis clearly showed that from the market success point of view, those firms that have the capability to identify the "right" problem have a significant competitive advantage over rivals. In other words, a perfect solution to a "wrong" problem does not matter.

- **Systems evolve in the predominant direction.**
  The course of a system's evolution coincides with the delivery of ever-increasing performance while requiring fewer resources for providing that performance. The predominant direction of evolution can be expressed as the ratio of the sum of the functions delivered by a system (an embodiment of performance) to the sum of connections the system needs to establish for obtaining the resources required for achieving the functionality. This ratio titled the Coefficient of Freedom (any function empowers a system and makes it freer, while any connection increases its dependency and decreases freedom) is presented in Figure 2. The Coefficient embodies the business world concept of value: the greater the Coefficient, the greater the value delivered by a product or a service.

$$C_{Freedom} = \frac{\Sigma \ Functions}{\Sigma \ Connections}$$

Figure 2. Coefficient of Freedom

GTI foundation

Historical analyses of the evolutionary process for various systems (those listed earlier, as well as bicycles, glass making, baking equipment, welding, shopping, banking, the car, movie renting, publishing, the computer mouse, the car door hinge, safety airbags, etc.) clearly show the validity of the Coefficient of Freedom. It is universal, whether it is applied to products, processes, services, or various entities (both for-profit and not-for-profit) such as industries, markets, regions, etc.

Moreover, these analyses lead firmly to the conclusion that systems do not evolve randomly. The evolutionary cycle of all systems, regardless of their specific nature, is governed by the same set of natural laws that are completely independent of human will and desire, which is the major postulate of GTI, first defined in 1988. The natural law governing the process of evolution (growth and expansion) of various systems states "the direction of a system's evolution coincides with a continuously increasing degree of freedom of this system's Environment" and is thus titled the Law of an Increasing Degree of Freedom.

GTI major capabilities

Acceptance of the GTI foundation, which is existence of the natural laws governing the process of evolution, automatically leads to the following capabilities that are direct corollaries (natural consequences) of that acceptance.

- **The nature of a challenge (problem, failure)**
  The nature of any challenge/problem/failure experienced by a system is a deviation from the direction prescribed by the natural laws of evolution. Consider an analogy of disobeying the laws of traffic, which always elevates the risk and creates problems. Being able to efficiently identify the origins of problems, which are always a result of our choices, greatly improves our abilities to effectively address them by going to the root cause and restoring a "lawful" behavior.

- **The nature of success**
  On another hand, the nature of success is in obeying the "LAWS". There is no exception from this rule. Just as we must follow the laws of physical science when designing products or services, if we expect these products or services to work well, we must also follow the laws of evolution. Today's executives, whether they know it or not, follow these laws when they succeed. However, they do so intuitively, but not consistently or methodically, thus producing very mixed results. GTI articulates evolutionary laws and introduces a set of tools for working consciously and strategically within the laws.

- **The capability to forecast the future of evolution**
  Knowledge of a system location on the evolutionary curve, combined with knowledge of the evolutionary laws, allows any entity to forecast the system's (product, process, service, etc.) future with a great degree of precision.

- **The capability to objectively judge upcoming innovations**
  Existence of natural laws of evolution has enabled creation of the objective criteria for evaluating proposed innovations, the importance of such criteria being self-evident. At the time of working on a direct-current motor, Thomas Edison completely dismissed the efforts by George Westinghouse, stating that alternating current was nonsense and had no future. Every innovation improves a system, moving it along the evolutionary curve. Whether this move complies with the laws (or deviates from the laws) constitutes a criterion for evaluating the innovation.

Before concluding this section, it is vitally important to make two points. First, the emergence of GTI, the only scientific prescriptive theory of innovation, does not eradicate the innovation-related risk nor guarantees the certainty of predicted results. Just as any scientific theory, GTI is just a model of the reality, and as such is, by definition, incomplete. However, the emergence of science, as compared to the art, significantly improves the success odds, the process' robustness, and the consistency of practical results, which is surely true in the case of GTI as well.

Second, while understanding and agreeing that GTI (just as any other scientific theory) can and should be continually perfected, it, in principle, completely meets the criteria for a robust innovation methodology set at the beginning of this paper.

GTI: Range of Practical Applications

Within GTI, innovation is, first of all, defined as a method of value creation that consists of qualitatively changing the state of a system. Depending on a specific entity's need that requires application of the method of innovation, the GTI divides its applications into three major groups: a) Reactive Innovation, b) Proactive Innovation, and c) Improving/Creating Organizational Capabilities. These groups, as well as specific GTI applications and tools, are presented in Figure 3 below.

		Applications	Major Tools
Marketing Offering Based Applications	**Reactive Innovation** **Customer Value is Known**	1. A performance-based challenge 2. Cost reduction 3. Quality / reliability improvement 4. Innovation assessment 5. Failure prevention 6. Patent circumvention / patent protection against circumvention	1. RelEvent Diagram (Systems mapping/analysis) 2. Problem-Solution templates 3. Conflict strategies 4. Algorithm for a Conflict Elimination (ACE - 2006) 5. Failure prevention analysis
	Proactive Innovation **Customer Value is Unknown**	1. System evolution forecasting 2. Strategic innovations 3. Business applications, for example: • ID growth opportunities • Corporate turnaround • New business strategy / business model • Commoditization avoidance • Change assessment, incl. BD/OD, M&A	1. Evolutionary templates 2. Generic growth strategies 3. Value growth templates 4. Value matrix 5. Reactive Innovation set of tools
Entity Based Programs	**Improving / Creating Organizational Capabilities**	1. The "Innovation On Demand" capability 2. The "Strategic Innovation" capability 3. Corporate Innovation Management system 4. Design for Advantage™: the next generation of an NPD methodology 5. Total Sustainability™ capability and its deployment 6. Corporate Knowledge Management system 7. The Invincible Enterprise™ Program	1. All of the above 2. The program schedules, breakdowns, templates, metrics, and other relevant documents

Figure 3. GTI applications and tools

The first group of applications relates to the situation when the value for its respective market/customer is known, but an entity has not yet addressed it to the market's satisfaction, and a change in a system state (an innovation) is required. Since the need for a change is demanded by the market, and an entity must react to it, this group of various well-known applications is titled "Reactive Innovation".

The second group of applications relates to the situation when the market does not have complaints. The entity itself pursues a change in its offerings, so the prosperous future will be assured. In this case, the entity proactively seeks a change, thus this group of applications (primarily driven by the future business goals such as discovery of strategic opportunities and threats, discovery of growth avenues, etc.) is titled the "Proactive Innovation".

The third and final group of applications relates to the need of the entities to continually improve its competitive capability and all of its integral components. Specifically, the need for a qualitative change (i.e. innovation) continually arises at each stage of the system life cycle; therefore, an entity has to have the capability to do it on-demand.

Finally, it is important to notice that while the majority of the applications (**and all the tools**) from the first two groups were tested and have proven their effectiveness, the applications of the third group were tested only partially and largely remain theoretical claims.

IMPORTANT CONCLUSIONS

There are a few important remaining points that need to be presented before concluding the paper.

While no company can in principle survive (to say nothing about growing and prospering) over the long run under the current probability of success, GTI presents the definitive way out of this situation. I would like to emphasize though that GTI is not a quick fix for all your corporate problems and issues. It is, instead, a potent theory that, after being learned and deployed, is definitely capable of controlling the process of innovation, which would effectively work for any specific application. As a result, GTI is perfectly positioned to significantly contribute to any conceivable business objective requiring a change of the status quo, which makes everything presented in this paper very much relevant to the members of LSSC.

Another aspect of GTI that makes it and this paper relevant to the LSSC objectives is that development of systems (according to the Natural Laws of Evolution) is fundamentally LEAN, as the Coefficient of Freedom promotes the most effective and efficient use of resources while delivering the most important and relevant functionality.

Finally, emergence of GTI (just as any other scientific theory) transforms the capricious art (the Chaos) into an orderly routine. It makes what was random, complex, and unknown into the less complex, better known, and hence more predictable and manageable.

Acknowledgements

Before acknowledging the contribution of individuals to the creation of GTI, it is my great honor and privilege to state that what is known today as GTI was started as a research project within the domain of the Theory of the Solution of Inventive Problems [7 - 9], presently known worldwide as TRIZ. Moreover, many of the TRIZ central concepts were used by me in the process of creating GTI, and even though the content of the majority of them has been ultimately changed, I feel strongly that TRIZ influence must be recognized and acknowledged.

Now I would like to acknowledge contribution of the following individuals:

- Genrich S. Altshuller, the late father of TRIZ, who encouraged the original research
- Alexander A. Malinovsky (Bogdanov), the late father of Tectology (1920) [10]
- Dr. Lev L. Velikovich (Belarus), a close friend and mentor, who was the first to recognize the importance of GTI and wholeheartedly encouraged the author
- Dr. John Terninko, a close friend and an intellectual sparring partner
- Greg Frenklach (Israel), a partner in the original research project
- My countless TRIZ colleagues, whose works contributed to my upbringing
- Last but not least, my family (wife Larisa Yezersky; our sons Geoffrey, Andrew, and Alexander; my parents Abraham Yezersky and Fira Yezersky), whose unconditional love and support allowed me to pursue the goal of creating GTI.

To all these individuals I owe my sincere appreciation and gratitude!

REFERENCES

[1]   Arie de Geus (April 1997). *"The Living Company"*, Harvard Business School Press, ISBN-10: 087584782X

[2]   W. Chan Kim, Renee Mauborgne (Boston, 2005). *"Blue Ocean Strategy"*, Harvard Business School Press ISBN 1-59139-619-0

[3]   Clayton Christensen, Michael Raynor (2003). *"The Innovator's Solution"*, Harvard Business School Press ISBN: 1-57851-852-0

[4]   Frost & Sullivan (2008.) *"New Product Development"*. Growth Process Toolkit. Retrieved from http://www.frost.com/prod/servlet/cpo/178024303.

[5]   Steve Schoenherr, Recording Technology History, notes. Retrieved from http://history.sandiego.edu/GEN/recording/notes.html

[6]   Glyn Davies (1996). *"A history of money"*. University of Wales Press. ISBN 0708317170

[7]   G. S. Altshuller (1984). *"CREATIVITY AS AN EXACT SCIENCE: The Theory of the Solution of Inventive Problems"*. Gordon and Breach. ISBN 0-677-21230-5

[8]   Genrich Altshuller (1999). *"The innovation algorithm"*. Technical Innovation Center. ISBN 0964074044

[9]   Genrich Altshuller (1996). *"And suddenly the inventor appeared"*. Technical Innovation Center. ISBN 0964074028

[10]   Alexander A. Bogdanov (Malinovsky). (1989) *"Tektologia"*, Economika Publishing House, Moscow. In Russian. ISBN 5-282-00538-7

www.ingramcontent.com/pod-product-compliance
Lightning Source LLC
Chambersburg PA
CBHW060601060326
40690CB00017B/3784